Strong Family Ties

THE TINY HAWKINS STORY

AS TOLD TO
Debra L. Winegarten
Ruthe Winegarten

PUBLISHER
SocioSights Press
AUSTIN, TEXAS

A SOCIOSIGHTS PRESS PUBLICATION

Published by
SocioSights Press
P.O. Box 1662
Austin, Texas 78767-1662

Photo Credits
All photographs are from the collection of Dr. Tiny Hawkins, except as indicated below:

Cover: Tiny Hawkins with resident Emma Winn, age 112. Photo by John Rhodes. Courtesy, *Dallas Morning News*, May 31, 1987, p. F-1.

p. 4: Courtesy Loretta P. Crudupt.

p. 22: Photo by Dorothea Lange. Courtesy Photographs and Prints Divisions, Schomborg Center for Research in Black Culture, The New York Public Library, Astor, Lenox and Tilden Foundations.

p. 30: The old Dallas County Courthouse. From the Collection of the Texas/Dallas History and Archives Division, Dallas Public Library, Image # PA83-25/1.

p. 74: Courtesy African American Museum of Dallas, Black Women's History Archives.

p. 96: Photo by Dana Byrum, Austin, Texas.

© Copyright 1998 by Leona T. Hawkins.

All rights reserved. No part of this book may be reproduced or transmitted in any form or by any means, electronic or mechanical, including photocopying, recording, or by any information storage or retrieval system, without the written permission of the Publisher, except where permitted by law. For information address: SocioSights Press, P.O. Box 1662, Austin, Texas 78767-1662.

ISBN: 0-9610340-9-2
Printed in the United States of America

Library of Congress Cataloging-in-Publication Data

Strong family ties : the Tiny Hawkins story / as told to Debra L. Winegarten,
　　Ruthe Winegarten
　　　　p.　　cm.
　　Consists of interviews by and about Tiny Hawkins.
　　Includes bibliographical references (p.).
　　ISBN 1-9610340-9-2
　　1. Hawkins, Tiny—Interviews.　2. Afro-American women—Texas—Dallas—Biography.　3. Afro-Americans—Texas—Dallas—Biography.　4. Nursing home administrators—Texas—Dallas—Biography.　5. Hawkins family—Interviews.
6. Dallas (Tex.)—Biography.　I. Hawkins, Tiny.　II. Winegarten, Debra L.
III. Winegarten, Ruthe.
F394.D2153H397　1998
976.4'281200496073'0092—dc21
　[B]　　　　　　　　　　　　　　　　　　　　　　　　　　　　　98-28400
　　　　　　　　　　　　　　　　　　　　　　　　　　　　　　　　　　CIP

The Rev. Deion Sanders with Tiny Hawkins

Founding Members, Dallas Chapter, National Council of Negro Women

*Special thanks to Betty Ragland, Ruth Butler, Romenia Montgomery,
Katherine Weems, Ruth Jones, Bishop H. W. and Gerldine Murph, Dorothy Harris,
John Wiley Price, Willis Johnson, Deion Sanders, Victor Ortiz, Royce West,
Steve Ladd, Cuz'n Lenny, Dewayne Carraway, John Ware, Al Lipscomb,
Diana Ragsdale, Eddie Bernice Johnson, Lymon and Bernice Washington,
Yvonne Ewell, Kathryn Gillium, Kathryn Wyatt,
Herbie K. and Joyclyn Johnson, Johnnie Taylor, Bobbie Patterson, Roosevelt Wheeler, Ken Carter,
Jim Washington, Dr. Harry Robinson, Arthur Busby, Charles English, Hiram and Gwen Harrison,
Jane Jones, Dickie Foster, Carlotta Wheeler, Evelyn and Jewell Meshack, George and Ada Willis,
Ada Williams, George Badget, Herbert Hawkins, Doris Bluett, Claudia Slesinger,
Bertha Holland, Richard and Bessie McGrady, Daisy Smith,
The Lewis' (Aretta, Brenda, Farley, Wayne and Marshawn), Mr. and Mrs. Harold Avery,
Mr. and Mrs. William Betts, Carrie Coleman, Felicia Agent, Dorothy Cox, Eldonna Whiteley,
Mr. and Mrs. Allen Madison, Mr. and Mrs. Walter Wilson, Mable White, Betty Lynn,
Abner Coit, Donna Johnson, Daisy Smith, Mr. and Mrs. Bill Lewis, Julia Jordan, and
Drs. Princess Jackson, Louis Deere, Herbert Chambers, Larry Lundy, Ben Clark,
Dan Jones, Claude Williams, Donald Ellis, and Irby Hunter.*

Women leading the way: Dallas Chapter, National Council of Negro Women

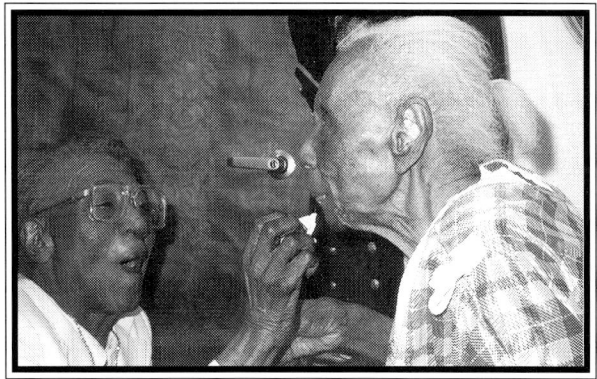

"I've done nothing on my own.
Only by the grace of God have I been able to make it this far.
Life has been a struggle, there has not been a "golden stairway,"
but one mountain after another staring me in the face.

Don't get me wrong, I don't regret any of the "toils and snares"
that have entangled my life because they have served me well.
They have proven to be the strengthening building blocks; staffs of life.

I never asked God to move a mountain,
only to give me the strength to climb it.
I never took the smooth side of the mountain and as I look back,
I know that I would not have been able to come this far
had I not had the "hand holds" on the rough side.

I have to turn aside every day that I am blessed to live,
to give thanks to God for the faith He has given me,
and for His "Amazing Grace."

TINY HAWKINS

*For my parents,
Frank and Willie Mathis,
who gave me my faith in God*

CONTENTS

STRONG FAMILY TIES

1	I care about people	9
2	A family that sticks together	15
3	We were all color blind, race didn't matter	23
4	I'll tell your fortune for a quarter	31
5	My husband said he wanted six kids	37
6	I didn't hold no long PTA meetings	47
7	I was like a rabbit in a briar patch	51
8	Losing a child was the worst thing	57
9	It's a family affair	65
10	I wouldn't give up	73
11	Leave no one behind	79
12	My strength is in God	83
	Epilogue	89
	Chronology	93
	Bibliography	97

Tiny was always the ram in the bush that
helped us to survive. Had it
not been for her, we would not be here today.
She has a special place in my heart.

CHAPTER ONE

"I CARE ABOUT PEOPLE"
TINY'S ETHIC OF CARE

She's the most giving person I've ever met in my life.
She helps any and everybody who comes through.
Rodney Hawkins

TINY HAWKINS:

If I see somebody that needs help, I'll give it to them

I will do anything for anybody to relieve human suffering. That's the missionary part of my mother coming out in me. She was active in the missionary society at the church. In those days when I was a girl, if anybody was sick in the neighborhood, the women of the church society would hold a prayer meeting, take up an offering of 25 or 30 cents and donate it to that family. They'd kill a hog, take them some food out of their garden, go to their house, cook a meal, clean up, and wash their clothes.

People don't do that kind of thing anymore, they really don't. But that's the kind of missionary work I do on a daily basis. Missionary work is personal with me. If I see somebody that needs some help, I'll give it to them.

"I'm like Jesus — you never know when I'm coming — so you had better be ready"

One time I came to the nursing home late Sunday afternoon. Nobody expected me to be in the facility at that particular time. I made rounds as usual, and I didn't like what I saw. I went through the building and saw the staff weren't doing their jobs. I found residents with urine on them that somebody could have been taking care of. One staff member was even laying up on the nurses' station when I walked in, and she couldn't get down. And the rest of them were sitting around the nurses' station.

So I got on the phone. I called my sisters, brothers, cousins, friends. Told them to please come over here and help me take care of these residents because I was getting ready to clean house. After I got enough people in here to take care of 'em, I fired the whole shift, nurses, aides, and all. I sure did, every last one of 'em. I wrote everybody's check and said, "Now, go on."

And I don't do that often. You've got to be pretty bad for me to fire you. I'll bet I haven't fired 25 people in the 30 years I've been here. You got to really push my button for me to do that 'cause I like to sit down and counsel with you, find out what your problems are, and see if we can't work them out.

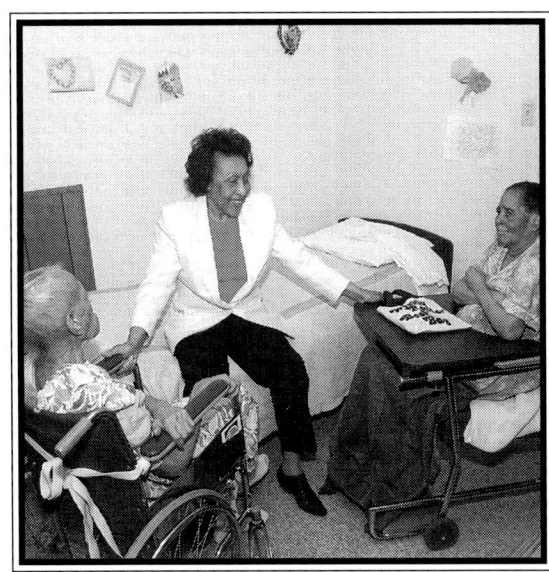

Nobody, nobody likes to be in a nursing home, and nobody likes to put their parents or a family member in a nursing home.

But when I fire you, I have had it up to here, so you've got to go. I have to fire you on the spur of a moment. You see, there's no excuse for not taking care of the residents; so you don't need to be in my employ. You don't represent me.

TINY HAWKINS:
I care about people

And that is one of the main reasons why I'm in this building, and the Lord knew, too, that I was going to have to take care of a lot of folks. That's the reason why He blessed me. It's not of my doing, it's of His, to bless me with a place where I'm able to take care of them.

I believe in strong family ties, I really do. I go and do what I can for my family members. And then when you're up and on your feet, I don't have time to be bothered. All my aunts and uncles, my mother, too, have died here at the nursing home. You reach a point in life where you can't take care of them at home.

Nobody, nobody likes to be in a nursing home, and nobody likes to put their parents or a family member in a nursing home.

But sometimes you don't have a choice. And I have met that challenge more than once in my life with my mother, all my aunties, even Aunt Arelia, the one who lived in Kemp until 1996 to the age of l06. She used to be such a hellion, but she's mellowed down a lot.

TINY HAWKINS:
She started crying — she had nobody, nobody

Before I owned the South Dallas Nursing Home, I worked there as the activity director. The money I was earning wasn't all that important. What really made me decide to stay was one little patient in Room 108. She was a cardiac patient; she was white. She had no family, she had nobody, nobody. Her doctors let her have three cigarettes a day, and I would take them to her. At that time, I was smoking, and we would smoke the cigarettes together.

One Wednesday I told her, "I'm going home, and I'll see you Monday." And she started crying. She said, "The days are so long without you. I don't know whether I'll be here Monday when you get back." And I sat there, and we talked, and I said, "I'll be back." I came back the next two days just to smoke a cigarette with her. It made her so happy for me to be there. I could see so many needs for both white and black residents there that were not being met. So that was my decision to stay.

JULIETTE HAWKINS WESLEY: (Tiny's third daughter)
Take care of the family

The specific words that her dad left with

her were, "Take care of the family. Keep them together." That's an enormous task at any period, especially to have it put on you when the family is so large.

He apparently thought he had reached the one child of his 12 who could take on that responsibility. And he was right. He apparently believed that, "You have more of me in you, and you've exemplified more of a leadership in the whole family, so you do that."

Granny would always listen to you.
I can't remember her getting mad.

LILY GREEN: (Bookkeeper and long-time friend)
Tiny's not selfish

I'd call it stick-to-it-ness. Whatever Dr. Hawkins got before her, she's determined to get it accomplished. What motivates everybody to get in and work with her is because she's a determined person. She's not selfish either. She wants to see others have as well as she has. She's the type of person you can love. Whenever you're at your lowest point, you can sit down and talk to her. And she really doesn't even have to know you. You can come in and ask something of her, and she will try to help you.

PORTIA SAMUELS: (Tiny's great-niece)
**She was always the
ram in the bush**

I can remember when Mama, Mattie Helen Samuels, was a single parent trying to raise me and my two brothers. I'm the baby and the only girl. The closeness of Aunt Tiny and Mama — Tiny helped to provide a home for us. She gave the financial support to this family. When Mama was struggling and working two jobs to try to put us through school and give us the bare necessities, Aunt Tiny was always the ram in the bush that helped us to survive. Had it not been for her, we would not be here today. She has a special place in my heart.

RODNEY HAWKINS: (Tiny's younger son)
She'll do anything for anybody

She's the most giving person I've ever met in my life. She helps any and everybody who comes through who looks like they want to do better or help themselves. She's always there for them through advice or financially. She'll give anybody a job. She tries to help everybody in the community. Religiously, any kind of way — you name it.

DON BRODEN: (Tiny's grandson)
My grandma holds our family together

She takes everybody under her wing, everybody. Right now she's employing people she doesn't have to. She could close the nursing home or sell it tomorrow and still be all right, but she doesn't. She keeps it open for the love of people. She's my grandmother, and I love her.

To our family, she is the center point. If one of us gets into an argument with a aunt or an uncle and says, "I don't want to talk to him

There were enough of me and my sisters that we kept shifts at the nursing home so someone was always with Mother before she died. Here we are coming from her funeral.

Ethel Livingston, Evelyn Dillworth, Ann Nelson, Tiny Hawkins, Leola Flewellen

anymore," she's not having that. She'll bring us all together: "We are family, and we have to stick together." But she's not only like that with family. She takes anybody under her wing.

The secret to her success is her heart. She really cares about people. It's something you got to be born with. You got to have a good heart. If you don't have a good heart, nothing will go right for you. Her heart's really right, and her faith in her religion is right.

TINY HAWKINS:

One of my favorite proverbs

Where there is no vision,
The people perish.
A vision without a task is a dream.
A task without a vision is drudgery.
A vision and a task
is the hope of the world.

THE TWIG STORY

TINY HAWKINS:
When one is down

I remember one thing my daddy told me that I'll never forget. At that time, it was ten of us living, and we were setting on the back steps. It was springtime in Kemp. He told me to go and get 20 switches from the hedges. They were thin. I went and got them and stripped them down. And he took ten on one side, and he took ten on the other side. He broke one until he broke ten. He gave each child a switch and said, "Break it." And they did. Then he took the other ten, and he plaited them together. And when those other ten switches were plaited and tied together, none of us that was setting there listening to him could break it. He said, "That's the way family ties are. Whatever happens to you kids, always stick together. When one is down, the other needs to be there to pick that one up."

I've always tried to do that. We have been a family that when one gets down, the rest of us are there until you get up and get on your feet.

EVELYN DILLWORTH: (Tiny's older sister)
You pick him up and carry him on

It's a funny thing about our family. We've been so close all these years. Times were hard back then. I remember once my father would always put us in the center of the floor, and he would be in the middle. He would get straws or sticks or little twigs. He'd give each one of us a twig to break. When we got through doing that, he'd say, "Now give 'em back." And we'd give 'em back, so then he plaited them. And he told us, "See, I can't break these."

"This is the way I want you all to be in coming up together. When one is down, the other one's down. You pick him up and carry him on. Don't ever forsake your sister or your brother. You stick together regardless of what comes or what happens."

EMMA JEAN WHITE: (Tiny's oldest sister)
It's a tie you can't break

My father would have a prayer every Sunday morning at the table. He got a big handful of sticks one time and he says, "I want you all to always stick together. One get in trouble, the whole family's in trouble." And he says, "If you stick together," and he took those sticks like this [shows with her hands they are in a bundle] and he couldn't break them. He says, "If you stick together, you won't never break the family tie." And we all, one get in trouble, all of us in trouble. One gets sick, all of us is probably sick. She (Tiny) was in the hospital about a month, I was in the hospital. And then I had another sister, she was sick. And that's just the way we go. One gets sick, it just goes on down the line. It seems like it's a tie that you can't break, that we all live like that.

We have been a family that when one gets down, the rest of us are there until you get up and get on your feet.

My grandmother Sally Mathis was a slave.
She was 104 years old when she passed.
We have always been a family that
when one gets down,
the rest are there until you get up and get on your feet.

CHAPTER TWO

A FAMILY THAT STICKS TOGETHER CANNOT BE BROKEN

TINY'S PARENTS: FRANK MATHIS (1884-1952) AND WILLIE MATHIS (1888-1983)

This is the way I want you all to be in coming up together.
That is the way family ties are. Whatever happens to you kids, always stick together.
Whenever one is down, the other needs to be there to pick that one up.
Frank Mathis

TINY HAWKINS:
My daddy was a preacher

My daddy, Frank Mathis, was a preacher. I believe like him, that we build on a strong family. Before he died I promised him that I was going to keep the family together.

Over the period of some 40-odd years since his death, I have tried to keep them together--the aunts and uncles, the brothers and sisters and nieces and nephews, the kids and the grandkids. I've tried to keep a strong family relationship.

TINY HAWKINS:
Yeah, daddy was a rebel

They all respected my daddy in Kemp. He kept shotguns around to protect the family and had an act of getting his shotgun. He really laid it on the line and backed it up with his shotgun, too. I don't know whether they respected him or his shotgun. No, he never had to use it, but he would sure get it. I got two of his old shotguns and one of my husband's.

Once a new white guy came into the community who was looking for somebody to wash and iron for him. He knocked on our door, and he asked my daddy could my mother or some of his girls do his laundry? And it just infuriated my daddy. My daddy told him, "Now, your wife might wash for mine, but mine's not going to wash for yours." Daddy give him a good cussing and got his shotgun and told him to get off his porch and don't come back.

TINY HAWKINS:
My daddy was a very prominent man

My daddy was on the school board in Kemp ever since I can remember. Well, he wasn't on it officially, but they would not think of hiring a black teacher without his okay.

The longer I live, I wonder what did everybody think about him. He was a very intelligent man, and he was highly respected. White people just loved him. Right now when we go down there to visit, they love us, too. They always say, "That's those Mathis' girls."

My father, Frank Mathis, and his sister, Cardie.

TINY HAWKINS:
I was a lot like my daddy

My daddy and I clashed over everything because we were too much alike. I think it was because I was born on his birthday, June 5th. And being his birthday present, I had the same characteristics that he had. I was like him, bullheaded, strong, and I have a lot of his features. My mother used to say that I walked like him. Basically, I kind of look like him, too.

One time we clashed over feeding the dog. I was about eight or nine, maybe ten, sitting on the back steps, and my daddy came out. I remember it 'cause I've never forgotten that whupping he gave me. He said, "Go feed the dog." I said to myself, "I'm not going to feed that little black son-of-a-bitch." I wasn't really intending for him to hear me.

And he said, "What did you say?" And I repeated it. Every time he asked me, I would repeat it, and he said, "You're going to feed it." And I said, "No," and he had a little old whip, and he hit me one time with it, and he said, "Go feed him." And I wouldn't. I told him, "No, I am not going to do it." He hit me six more times, and I still wouldn't. And then he just went crazy on me.

Then my mother came to the door. That was the first time that I had ever heard my mother call my daddy by his name. He always called her "Sweetheart," and she called him "Baby." She said, "Frank, don't hit her again. Because if you do, you'll kill her, she will not do it. She's just like you. Now don't hit her anymore." And he just folded his whip up, threw it down, and went on back. He wanted somebody to stop him.

Oh, I rolled in the dirt, I was just a holy mess. My sisters put me in a tub of water and washed me off and greased me with some Vaseline. I wouldn't speak to him for a week. I just cut him to death with my eyes.

EMMA JEAN WHITE: (Tiny's oldest sister)
Tiny and my father were exactly alike

See, I was the oldest and I had to tend to all

of them because my mother was sickly. I had to take care of the whole family ever since I was eight years old. Wash, iron and everything else. Go tell Tiny to do something, she's hard-headed like my daddy was. They would tangle, they were both just alike. Time after time, they'd have their arguments.

She'd always win because he'd just walk on off and leave her because he knew she was just like him and she wasn't going to give up. She's going to have the last word. Otherwise, she was just as sweet and nice as she could be. She was willing to help anybody, didn't matter who it was, she helped you. But she was like him, when she said something, she meant it. That was it.

FRANK MATHIS, JR.: (Tiny's younger brother)
All of us were a close-knit family

As Tiny grew up, she was a competitor. If I wanted to play basketball, she wanted to play basketball. If I played anything, she wanted to play, too.

I got Tiny in trouble once. My dad, a blacksmith, had a shop with a forge that burned coal in a blazer. Dad was going downtown and told me not to touch it, said that when he came home, I could turn it on.

When Tiny came home, I said I wanted to show her something, so I lit the forge and it blazed up. Dad came home while I was in the middle of turning on the forge. He was really mad. He told Tiny not to let me or anyone else lead her into doing something because it might be wrong.

I was punished for disobeying him, Tiny not much. Tiny always had special privileges because she was born on Dad's birthday. Mama was soft-hearted, all wrapped up with the boys, whereas our dad was wrapped up with the girls.

TINY HAWKINS:
My daddy took care of us

I never heard him call my mother by her name. When one of us kids was sick during the night, my mother never got up with us. Daddy would say, "Sweetheart, that's all right. Lay back down; I'll see about the kids. I'll take care of them." If one of us would cough, he'd call us by our name, and he was up just like that. He was constantly getting up, tucking us under the cover. We never got up in a cold house, 'cause he'd always get up before day and make a fire in the wood heaters so the house would be warm when we got up. We had a beautiful father.

We always had arts and crafts, and he always had some type of philosophy to give to us. He said, "I might not be here to see it, but before the end of time, you can be sitting in your living room, and you'll be able to see what is going on in London, England." The first TV I saw reminded me that this is what my daddy had predicted.

And he would read a biblical scripture and interpret it. Once he said, "Before the end of time, like the mark of the beast in the Book of Revelations, you're going to have to have a number before you can get anything." I remember when they rationed sugar, he had been talking about the numbers and the stamps that you would have to have. And he'd say, "I may not be here to see these things, but they will come to pass." And every day in the nursing home I'm always asking somebody, "What is your Social Security number, what is your Medicare number or your Medicaid number?" And then I think about my daddy.

TINY HAWKINS:
My daddy was a very wise man

He only had a third grade education, but he never stopped studying. You would have thought that he was a college professor. He helped us with our geometry, our algebra, our everything when we were going to school. Just to talk to him or be around him, everybody thought that he did have a college education.

He grew up in the Wills Point, Forney area, about 30 miles east of Dallas. He had to do most of his studying by lamp light. He had a pretty rough life growing up, but he stressed education with us. Although a lot of times we couldn't go to school because we had to help with the farming, at night we had to study our lessons. And we had to recite them before him, and when we went back to school, we were way ahead of our class.

My daddy built the Glasco Chapel AME Church in Kemp where he was the minister. We were African Methodists. Oh, he didn't make much money as a minister. I remember one time when I was a little kid, the congregation took up an offering, and it was a $1.36. And one of the trustees or stewards said, "Let's make it a dollar-and-a-half," and my daddy said, "No. Nobody takes an after-offering in my church. This is God's house. What was given was given from the heart. Anything else is man, and I don't want it, and I don't need it." So he wouldn't let them collect another 14 pennies to make it a dollar-and-a-half.

He grew up basically without a mother or a father. From the time he was about 11 or 12 years old, I think he just made it on his own. They said his daddy was an Indian, so he didn't know too much about him. Whoever you worked for you took their name. And that was the name his mother took, Mathis, Sally Mathis. My sister said that some white people raised our daddy, and that's where he got the name of Frank Mathis.

EMMA JEAN WHITE: (Tiny's oldest sister)
She was 104 years old

My grandmother, Sally Mathis, I never seen her but once and when she passed, we were living back out in the country. My daddy had bought a farm out in the country and we lived out there. But they say she was 104 years old when she passed.

TINY HAWKINS:
Mother and me

They say when my daddy died, white and black came from all over Kaufman County to the funeral in Kemp. The burying grounds was 19 or 20 miles from town. The procession was so long that when the hearse pulled up in Egypt, Texas, for the burial, the last car was just leaving Kemp, that's how long the procession was.

For a long time after my daddy died, I felt my mother did not treat me the way she was treating the other girls. She would go spend the night with them, but with me, never. And if we'd all be in a room together, and I'd come in and start talking, she'd get up and leave. And I got the feeling that maybe it was for being my daddy's favorite child.

That's the way I felt until I had enough. After my father had been dead maybe a year, I just about had all of my mother I could take. I loved her dearly, but I couldn't understand the way she was. I'd asked her to come spend the night with me, she wouldn't come. So I had it out with her. I said, "Mama, I do not feel since Papa's been dead that you treatin' me like you do Evelyn and Ethel, Leola, and Jean. You never come to see me, you never spend any time with me. We can all be in a room, and if I walk in, you'll get up and leave. I want to know the

Maloney Eldridge, our mother's mother

reason why. Is it that I was the favorite child, and you just don't care about me since he's been dead, or what?"

And she started crying, and she said, "No, you are so much like your daddy that I just cannot stand to be around you. Until I get over his death, I don't know whether I can stay around you. You walk like him, you talk like him, you even say some of the words that he said. It's just rough on me." So we hugged and cried together. And for awhile I kept my distance. It took her about two years, and then we finally became real close together again.

We was coming from my brother's funeral the other day, and I said, "Mama was pregnant for 24 years straight. That was 24 years." Because she had one of us every two years. She spent a good part of her adult life being pregnant, and she looked good when she passed.

ANN NELSON: (Tiny's younger sister)
My daddy always had good credit

Sometime during the wintertime there's no work for farmers out in the country. I remember once Daddy went in the kitchen, and there wasn't any corn meal around.

He went to the store in town and told the white store owners, "I don't have any money, but I need food for my family. And when summer comes, I will pay you back," and so they let him have the food. You know, if they had not given him the food or let him have it on credit, he was going to take it anyhow. He wasn't coming back home without some food for his kids. That's why he had a gun. Fortunately, he never had to use his gun that way.

ETHEL LIVINGSTON: (Tiny's older sister)
Tiny has ways like our father

I considered my father a person like the biblical prophet Amos, a farmer and a preacher. We lived on a 90-acre farm and grew up with religious parents who were very strict on us. I think the white people respected him because he would not take a back seat, he would just tell you what he thought. If he called for a fight, I was right there. Whatever he did, I would do, too, because I felt like it was the right thing to do. I believed everything he said. If he said it to me, that's just the way it was. Because he was my father, I respected him, I thought there was no other person like him.

Our father was very kind, fine. Tiny is like him. She has ways like him. She tells you exactly what she thinks. When she has enough of anything, she has enough. She doesn't brood: what comes up, comes out. When she's through with you, she's through with you. And my father was the same way.

EMMA JEAN WHITE: (Tiny's oldest sister)
We always prayed together

See, Tiny was born on my father's birthday and every year that he lived, he'd have all of us together and we would have prayer, reading of the Bible and all.

After he died, we asked Tiny not to have it no more because we thought we just couldn't handle it. But the first year, she had it, and my baby brother, he was reading the Bible and I looked down and his hands looked just like my daddy's hands. I ran out the back door, and my daddy was kind of a carpenter, fixed things.

When I run out the back door, I looked down and he had made Tiny an ironing board. And everywhere I went, I could see him in things that he had done. That's why we asked her not to have it anymore, and she didn't for a long time.

TINY HAWKINS:
I still have this little birthday ritual

My siblings wanted me to stop our praying together. I still do it, I do it religiously on my birthday. I go in the bathroom, read a scripture, have my prayer, sing my little old song, and come on out. I do it by myself because it upsets the family so much. It was tradition in the family, and I've never stopped.

TINY HAWKINS:
My niece was raised just like she was one of us

My niece, Mattie Helen, was like a sister to us, growing up in our house. Mama raised Mattie Helen right along with us.

Even though she's my niece, I'm only five years older than she is. Mattie Helen is actually older than her Aunt Ann by 13 months. Mattie Helen's still like our sister. Ann says she feels just as close to her as her own sister, it's no different. We were raised together.

MATTIE HELEN SAMUELS: (Tiny's niece)
Grandma was a homebody

My grandfather was a wonderful man. He bought all my grandmother's clothes, he bought the groceries. She never went to town to even buy a pair of socks. She never went to a store to buy nothing. She was that shy she just didn't want to go. She'd just cook, feed her children, stay at home, keep house, an immaculate housekeeper. Thank God for her 'cause she taught me how to do it. She was just a wonderful lady, she was a doll.

My grandmother had a bread pan about a foot wide and two feet long. When I was a child, I would make biscuits in that pan. I was cooking for the whole family. She'd sit in her chair and watch me and tell me what to do, and I did it. You know, that was in the country. You'd slice some ham off of the hock. You made your own bacon, you'd slice your bacon off the flat part of

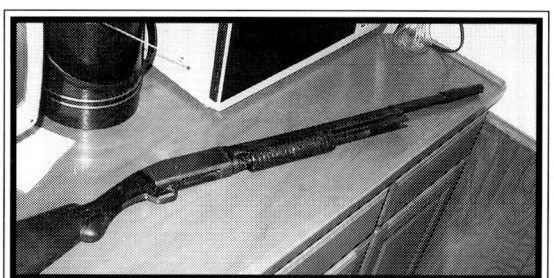

I dreamed about generations. You had a little kid with you.

the meat. It'd be so thick you didn't have to fry but five or six pieces, and you had enough for six people. We had the sausage stuffed off in the gut of the hog. Just break it off and drop it in the skillet. Boy, that was some good eating. We had biscuits and homemade molasses, we made our own sugar cane syrup. Cows, hogs, pigs, a whole barn. Chickens, guineas, ducks, turkeys, you name it, we had it, some of everything.

BURT HAWKINS: (Willie's grandson, Tiny's older son)
She had a way to talk to kids

I remember the last serious conversation that I had with my grandmother was while I was in the service. She told me, "I dreamed that you came in here, and you had a little kid with you. You was holding his hand."

I had had the mumps when I was young, and I wasn't supposed to be able to have kids. Lo and behold, before Granny died, Belinda got pregnant, and I got one.

She had a way to talk to kids that you could understand and realize that if you had done wrong, you really needed to stop. She'd say, "Don't make me get mad at you." I can't remember her ever getting mad.

Granny would always listen to you. She'd give you a little tidbit of her wisdom. She sit you down and just let you talk it out with her.

There's so much similarity between her and Mother, like when Mother sits me down and tries to tell me something that's going to do me some good. I see the very same mannerisms and the way that she talks as Grandmother.

When Grandmother was living, Grand would say, "Well, Tiny, you know that you ain't doing this," or "You need to do that," and Tiny'd go do it, no questions asked. That's the same way that me and the rest of us kids are about Mother. If that's what she wants us to do, just go on and do that.

I think the driving force was that hot sun,
the hot sun and the hard work. I can remember I hated it so bad.
The sun would bear down on you so.
Picking and chopping cotton wasn't my bag.

CHAPTER THREE

WE WERE ALL COLOR BLIND, RACE DIDN'T MATTER GROWING UP IN KEMP

*I think the driving force was that hot sun,
the hot sun and the hard work.
I knew I didn't want to do that the rest of my life.*
Tiny Hawkins

TINY HAWKINS:
How did I get the name "Tiny"?

I was born on June 5th, the ninth of 12 children. They said that when I was two months old, I weighed over 22 pounds, and they thought I had dropsy. They brought me to Dallas to the doctor, and he said it wasn't nothing but fat. So they started calling me Tiny.

TINY HAWKINS:
Education has always been one of my primary goals

I think the driving force was that hot sun, the hot sun and the hard work. I can remember I hated it so bad. The sun would bear down on you so. Picking and chopping cotton wasn't my bag. I knew I didn't want to do that the rest of my life. I said, "If I ever get out of the cotton patch, I ain't going back."

I always tried to figure out a way that I didn't have to work too hard. I didn't like to sew like my sisters, either. But I liked to read, and I liked to do things that they said couldn't be done. Something had to be a challenge to me. I felt like the only way that I wouldn't have to keep picking cotton was to get an education. I always had a craving for knowledge. I just wanted to learn. And I enjoyed reading and studying.

TINY HAWKINS:
That's how bad I hated it

I just wanted to go to school and I wanted to make me some money, and I didn't want to go to the cotton patch. I didn't like it, didn't want to do it. I didn't have a problem being at home, I didn't want to pick no cotton, chop it, nothing else. I said if I ever got away, I wasn't going back. I said, "If the cotton boll was a rattle snake and it crawled up in my lap, I'd just tell him to get on," that's how bad I hated anything to do with cotton. No, Lord.

EMMA JEAN WHITE: (Tiny's oldest sister)
They would always argue about picking cotton

Tiny did not like to work in the field. She and my father would get to arguing about it, and sometime I guess if the good Lord hadn't stepped in, they might have went to fist city. Because she was just as stubborn as he was. But the good Lord stepped in and changed him. But now, she didn't give in, he'd just walk on off, let her have it. But she did not like the field work. And I can't blame her for it because I used to do it, and I did it all my life.

She just wanted to stay at the house when she was a child and play. She wanted to have a good time. She wasn't going to work in that field. And I couldn't blame her, because it was hard, hard work. I used to have to go there and pick 400 and 500 pounds a day, come back home, cook two meals a day, and that's how I made my living. I did that when my daddy was living.

First time I married, I didn't love that man. I just married him to get away from home, because I was tired of working so hard.

My daddy was a very, very strict man. He thought if he told you to jump, you supposed to say, "How high?" He was very, very strict.

TINY HAWKINS:
One of our cousins was the teacher

Our elementary school had three or four rooms. The white school was just a little bit bigger than ours. We were on one end of town, and they were on the other end. We had maybe 35 or 40 students in our school.

One of our cousins, Pearlie Trammel, was the teacher. My last two years in school, 1936-38, we had two men teachers that came from out of town, Mr. Cooper and Mr. Beachem. The principal was a black woman, Marva Sutton, who was a real inspiration to us.

TINY HAWKINS:
I wanted to learn

I wanted to learn, and anytime I couldn't get to school because I'd have to stay out to work or help out around the house, I would be angry. There was a boy in my grade school class who could go to school more than I could. He was so smart until I honestly hated him. If he stood at the head of the class one day, I'd stand there the next day. I was very good at reciting verses. I remember this poem I liked to say. It was called "A Psalm of Life" by Longfellow, and I still remember lots of the lines.

> Tell me not in mournful numbers,
> Life is but an empty dream! —
> For the soul is dead that slumbers,
> And things are not what they seem.
>
> Life is real!
> Life is earnest!
> And the grave is not its goal;
> Dust thou art, to dust returneth,
> Was not spoken of the soul.

TINY HAWKINS:
My daddy always made a good living for us

It was fun growing up in the country because we had our own farm. We worked hard in the summertime, had a nice crop, and saved up for the winters.

We'd pick cotton or pull corn or peas, okra, beets, tomatoes, and lettuce. We raised everything. There was always food. We ate good. Our daddy raised everything that we could eat, had plenty cows and pigs, and he fed everybody in the community out of his garden. We just had everything, including fairly decent clothes.

Papa had a garden. He had five acres of vegetables — tubs full of cucumbers, peppers, everything you could think of in the vegetable line, we had it. When fresh stuff came in, we'd still have cans left over from the last season. Mama would can 300-400 jars of food-peas, corn, tomatoes, beets, okra, everything that grows in the garden. My oldest sister Emma Jean still cans. The only things they bought were flour, sugar, coffee, baking soda, baking powder, sugar, and corn meal. We supplied the whole neighborhood.

When we all moved to Dallas, we'd go back to Kemp to get corn, new potatoes, greens, turnips, beets, tomatoes. Put them in the back end of the car. He supplied our kitchen even after we moved away from Kemp.

My mother made everything we wore. I really didn't know we were poor until somebody said we was, 'cause we had a lot of love. My daddy made pretty good money from cotton until the Depression came, and then we were poverty-stricken, they said. Didn't have no money. He lost most of everything he had.

Oh, we had a ball, growing up in that small town, we really did. We played ball. I love sports. I played basketball, and I played football and softball. They didn't have enough boys to make up a football team, and me and Bennie Fay, who is married to my cousin, Dallas Freeman, we'd suit up and play football with the boys. We were just as tough as they were.

TINY HAWKINS:
My daddy built the church on our property

The land is still there, but the church was demolished six or seven years ago. We still got that property down there now growing weeds. After everybody moved away, and my daddy passed, and my mother came up here to Dallas, our old family house got run down, and then it was torn down, too. My sister, Emma Jean, has another house on the property, and she still lives there. Aunt Arelia's house is down there, too.

We had three churches right in a row. We

Frank Mathis and his family in Kemp.

had an AME (African Methodist Episcopal), a CME (Colored Methodist Episcopal), and a Baptist. The Baptist had the most members, and we were AME, and I think the churches went by families. The Mathis, the Woods, the Earls — we were all Methodists. The Browns was all CME Methodists; Eldridge was members of the Baptist church. The Freeman family was a pretty big family, and they were also our first cousins.

The church was the only place in the country that we had to go to and visit each other, the family members, once a week on Sunday. That was one thing our parents insisted on — that you go on Sunday to church. Sometimes during the summer months we had bible school.

It was 34 of us first cousins in that little small town. My mother had eight girls and four boys. Her sister, Etta Freeman (that's where the Freemans come in), they were Baptist. Etta had eight boys and four girls. My mother's brother, Uncle Zimmie Eldridge, had eight kids. Uncle Jay Hugh Eldridge had two. So that made us have in that community 34 first cousins.

TINY HAWKINS:
Race didn't matter

There were lots more whites than blacks in Kemp, but I never felt segregated there. We may have been, but I didn't feel it, or I didn't know it. We just grew up together, the white and the black kids, and we'd fight each other, and then it was all over with. We didn't know one was white and the other one was black until somebody told us. Maybe we were sheltered, but I never felt a lot of segregation.

We had our own cafes, and the white folks had theirs. And we never bothered to go to theirs. One of the guys that I was raised up with is now president of Bank One down home. They'd eat at our house, or we'd eat at their house. This white family, our farms adjoined each other. We were friends.

ANN NELSON: (Tiny's younger sister)
We had lots of white friends

We all mingled together, Therese Nobles, Paul Hardy and them Dawson boys. Paul Hardy was real close to us, 'cause they used to come to our house, and we went to their house.

EMMA JEAN WHITE: (Tiny's oldest sister)
They took everything but our clothes

At one point, our daddy sold his place back out there in the country past Cedar Creek, and bought 90 acres in Kemp, and we all moved there. But then the Depression come on, and our daddy didn't make a good crop, and he couldn't pay the note. So Bush, the fellow he had bought the land from, foreclosed on him, took everything we had. We didn't have nothing left. Bush took the horses and the mules, plows, tools, everything 'cept our clothes.

Then daddy finally bought another place in Kemp close to where I live now. Then he bought still another place down the road, but when he got in bad health, he sold that one.

LEOLA FLEWELLEN: (Tiny's older sister)
My father was real smart

All of us were raised up in the country. It was really exciting and happy. Our daddy liked to hunt, him and his dog Jack. In the wintertime, he'd set out his hooks in the pond. He'd kill squirrels and shoot ducks, and I knew when he left home with his gun, he was going to bring us something good back to eat.

EMMA JEAN WHITE: (Tiny's oldest sister)
He was a butcher and a good blacksmith, too

You know, our daddy was a butcher. He made his living in the wintertime slaughtering animals for other people. He'd kill them, skin and scrape them and cut them up, and he would use salt to cure the meat with and whatever his potion was, he would make up and put it on there, too. Smoked where they had the large building, called it a smoke house, a fire would be built with certain types of wood.

He also was a blacksmith. He would file saws, he made files and all this kind of stuff, sharpen knives, he was the blacksmith in that area, shoe horses.

LEOLA FLEWELLEN: (Tiny's older sister)
We were the first blacks in town to have everything

We were such an ambitious family. We were the first blacks to have an ice box, then after there were wood heaters, we were the first to have gas and electricity, a telephone, running water. The first refrigerator we bought, everybody in the city came to see it.

I remember when I was about four or five years old, our daddy bought us a Victrola. It stood up on the floor, and you'd wind it up, and you put your record on there and then play it.

He didn't get nothing cheap. Anytime something new came out, he'd go to town, and the people there would always let him have these things he wanted. Because he'd tell you he would always pay you back. So we all are like that, if we get anything on credit, we pay, got good credit.

My father would always buy the best. Once he bought us a waterless cooker, and you could put those ducks in there. If you season them real good and clamp that lid down, they would cook without any water. It was like a pressure cooker.

After the horse and wagon, the first thing that came out was a buggy. Our daddy would always get a two-seater. They called it a surrey with this little old fringe around it. Now that's what he took us to school in. Even his horses had nice harnesses on them with pretty red tassels and gold shiny buttons.

LEOLA FLEWELLEN: (Tiny's older sister)
Lights that shine a hundred miles

The first car that I rode in, it was a T-model Ford. It belonged to us. It was a big old car, never will forget it, brown and long.

I was so excited about the bright lights. I put my hands on my hips, and I told my cousin, "You know what? The lights shine a 100 miles."

Frank Mathis on his front porch in Kemp, Texas.

She said, "No, not a 100 miles, a 100 yards." And I went and asked my daddy, I said, "Daddy, didn't you say our car lights shone a 100 miles?" He said, "No, baby, a 100 yards."

Then in 1923, when I was about eight, we got a Dodge. And every four or five years, we'd get another one. My daddy loved the Dodges.

LEOLA FLEWELLEN: (Tiny's older sister)
Our daddy protected his family

He invented a lot of things, and he made pretty things for us like cedar chests. He even made little old slots to lay his gun across where he kept it hung up on a rack.

He'd tell us, "That gun is nothing to play with, you don't bother it." He put it right where if anyone tried to harm his family, he could get to it. He protected his family in every way.

Basketball was my favorite sport at Kemp High School. I played forward, guard, every position there was. If we didn't beat them playing, we beat them fighting after the game, one of the two. All except Cross Roads, they were all bigger than us.

TINY HAWKINS:
I don't remember the Klan in Kemp

My sister Ethel was quite a bit older than me. Not long after I was born, she recalls an ugly incident involving the Ku Klux Klan. I don't remember anything about the Klan or any kind of violence in Kemp. My main memories are of that hot sun.

ETHEL LIVINGSTON: (Tiny's older sister)
I remember the Ku Klux Klan

I think I was about ten years old, that's the first time I remember the Ku Klux Klan. They had one of their meetings near our farm. We were sharecroppers. One of the white farmers there, his name was Jim Houston, told my daddy about the meeting that was going to be held above his (Houston's) house.

My daddy said, "Okay, anything y'all want to do, go ahead and do it. Just don't bother my family." And Jim Houston said, "Oh, Frank, you know they're not going to bother you." And I remember my daddy loading two or three shotguns across his lap.

Daddy said, "Now I'm going to tell you white people one thing. If you come down here, I'm not the only one that's going to leave. I'm going to take some of you with me. I got three or four shotguns here, and I've got a .38."

"You know me. I don't bother anybody. But if you come here messing with my family, and we're not doing anything to you, I'm going to leave some of you laying there. Now that's the way it is. You may get me, I'm sure you will, but I'm going to carry somebody with me."

They had their hoods on and their torches, and I remember seeing them burn the crosses up the street. But they did not come down and bother us at all.

I remember how some other white men beat up a black man named Louis Ratcliff, took him down in the woods and beat him. The white man's wife had asked Louis to play a game of 42 with her, all he did was play a game.

But they beat him, and the next day, Louis had to leave town. And the Youngbloods, some white people, they left with him, because they said that they could not stand to see anybody do a person like they did Louis Ratcliff.

ETHEL LIVINGSTON: (Tiny's older sister)
I was the first one to leave Kemp

They didn't have a high school in Kemp at the time I was growing up. After I finished grade school, I lived with my grade school teacher in her home in Terrell. She taught in Kemp, but lived in Terrell. So I stayed with her in Terrell, finished Burnet High School there.

I had just finished high school and had come back home. It wasn't long before I moved to Dallas in the early 1930s to work for the Threadgills. I was the first one of my family to leave Kemp and come to Dallas. The Threadgills were a white family who had lived in Kemp. And one weekend they came back to Kemp to visit their daughter who was married to Joe Everetts, he was in real estate. The Threadgills told me they wanted someone to come and work for them, and they picked me. So I just came back to Dallas with them.

I worked in another private home when I first came to Dallas in 1937, they were the Mauses, musicians who lived out on Mockingbird Lane. I worked for them for years.

ETHEL LIVINGSTON: (Tiny's older sister)
We are a closely-knitted family

I felt like I raised my whole family because when they left the little town of Kemp, they came to Dallas, and I just watched over them like they were my children. My sisters and brother, Evelyn, Leola, Tiny, Ann, Carnegie (who we called Tom), the whole Mathis family, when they came here, they came to me. Everyone would get settled, and then they went their separate ways.

Tiny lived with me a while when she first came to Dallas, and then we lived next door to each other for quite a few years, and her children was raised around me. I just took them as my family. I didn't think about having a family of my own until it was too late. I was too busy helping someone else with their children. I helped my sister Evelyn and Tiny, too. But we had a good life. We've always enjoyed each other; we are a closely knitted family.

As soon as we sat down, the judge said,
"You 'niggers' get up and get to the back." And
when he said that, I jumped up and moved to the front.
My sister caught ahold to me and was pulling me back.
By that time her lawyer came in, and both of them was pulling me, and
I drug both of them up to the bar.

CHAPTER FOUR

I'LL TELL YOUR FORTUNE FOR A QUARTER

*It's just been a close-knitted family.
Wherever one moved, one of the sisters or the
brothers would buy a house next door.*
Mattie Helen Samuels

TINY HAWKINS:

When I finished high school, I came to Dallas

In Kemp, I didn't get to go to school that much because sometimes we had to stay out to chop and pick cotton. Because it was 12 of us in the family, it was really, really very difficult for us to get an education. My daddy was a poor farmer and preacher.

I finished high school when I was almost 16 years old because I studied at night. After those days in the cotton fields, I decided to figure out a better way of doing things. Education has always been one of my primary goals.

I came to Dallas in 1938 to keep on with my education, but first I had to get a job. Ethel, one of my older sisters, was working for some big prominent rich people in Dallas, and they needed a maid. They had a maid, a chauffeur, a yard man, and Ethel was the cook. They had about half a dozen people who worked for them, and I was making $7.50 a week as the maid. All I did for them was clean up the house and wash the dishes after dinner.

I got room and board. I stayed in the little servant quarters with my sister, Evelyn, who was living there then. Out of the $7.50 I earned, I lived off $2.50, I saved $2.50, and the other $2.50 I used to pay my tuition to beauty school. I finished beauty school in 1940 before I was 18, so I had to wait a while before I could go to the State Board and get my beauty license. And while I was waiting, I worked part-time at the Progress Laundry. After I went to the State Board and got my beauty license, I started working in a beauty shop. Much later, in 1960, I earned an instructor's license in cosmetology.

TINY HAWKINS:

The Jordans were a very nice family

But I had several more jobs in between times trying to go to school. I worked for the Jordan family out on Lakewood. Miz Jordan was a very lovely person and was very fond of me.

I would always read a lot, and I had found a magazine where it said you could order some cards for 50 cents. And they would teach you how to read fortunes.

I ordered those cards, I studied that book, and I studied those cards. One evening Miz Jordan came down while I was washing dishes, and I said, "Miz Jordan, I know how to read fortunes." She said, "You do?" I said, "Yes. Let me read your fortune." So she said, "Okay." I cut the cards, and I was only repeating what the book said the cards meant. She said, "You know, that's true." And that spurred me. I said, "Oh, well, maybe these cards are right."

One day Miz Jordan had a bridge party. And she told everybody, "You know, Tiny can read your fortunes." So I had to read everybody's fortune with the cards, and she made everybody pay me a quarter. And eventually, I didn't do nothing but ride around in that limousine with her and read fortunes.

TINY HAWKINS:

One lady worked me so hard 'til the cotton patch looked good

Oh, I had some incidents in a lot of private homes that I wouldn't even care to mention because I acted so ugly. One lady out in Highland Park — I didn't work for her but one day. When I got to work that day I had to wash, I had to iron, cook, clean up, I had to do it all. I'd worked from about 7:30 that morning until 7:30 that night. The last thing she told me to do was to go upstairs and turn John's bed down. And I told her I wouldn't walk upstairs if Baby Jesus was up there to turn his bed down. I said, "And you give me my money now because I quit, and I will not be back."

She didn't want to pay me. It was only $1.25. I told her that as hard as I had worked, she would pay me, or she would pay somebody, so her husband came out and paid me. He gave me my car fare, and I left, and I didn't go back.

I had to get me an education.
I declared I wasn't going to work for nobody.

That woman worked me so hard until that was another reason why I felt like that I had to get me a education. I declared I wasn't going to work for nobody, that they was going to work for me.

TINY HAWKINS:

"Niggers" are supposed to do what I want done

I had a very bad incident one time with another lady that I worked for. She was an alcoholic, which I did not know at the time, and her husband was a high school teacher. I won't call their last names because they're very prominent people here in Dallas. They said as long as I took care of their kids not to worry about anything else. I had worked for them for about three weeks. And I was very, very fond of the kids, Nancy and Eric.

One evening the woman came into the kitchen, and I had both of the children sitting up on the counter. I was peeling some carrots for dinner that night; I had peas and carrots, mashed potatoes, and pork chops, that's what I was cooking when she came in. She said, "Why don't you have dinner done?" I said, "Because I haven't had an opportunity to get it done. I've been busy with the kids." She said, "Well, 'niggers' are supposed to do what I want done when I want it done, and I will slap the hell out of you if you don't get it done."

TINY HAWKINS:
I'll cut Mississippi on your ass

And I said, "I'll cut `Mississippi' on your ass and dot every `i' in it." And I started towards her with this knife in my hand. She ran out the back door, and I hit the screen. I ripped the screen with the knife 'til it hung halfway in the door. She ran up the street with me running up behind her. She went to Miss Juniper's house, and say she's going to call the police. I told her to call the whole damn force, I'd be there when they got there. And I stood out there in that yard. I wouldn't go in the lady's house.

I suddenly thought about those kids. I said, "Oh, my God, I left Nancy and Eric sitting on that counter." I ran back down to the house, and they were still sitting up there. So I finished cooking, took care of those kids, and when her husband came home, he wanted to know where his wife was. And I say, "She's up to Miss Juniper." He said, "What's she doing up there?" I say, "I run her up there." He said, "What on earth happened?" I said, "She called me a 'nigger', and she said she would slap me." And he said, "Oh, my God. She must have been drinking. Come on and get your clothes, and let me take you home."

So he took me home with the kids riding along in the car, and paid me for two weeks' work. He said if I needed any references to have them to call him at the high school where he was a football coach. But I didn't. About two weeks later, she called me on the telephone and wanted me to come back to work. And I said, "You don't want me to come back to work." She said, "Yes, I do, we got a good understanding." I said, "No, we don't, because the next time I may catch you, and I'll be sorry the rest of my life. You don't want me to come back to work."

TINY HAWKINS:
Every year she sent me a dollar for my birthday

You know, she sent me a dollar on my birthday and for Christmas until she lost track of where I was. But I never went back. She'd always send me a birthday card and a Christmas card from Nancy and Eric, and a dollar would always be in it, every year.

TINY HAWKINS:
I didn't know what segregation was until I came to Dallas

In Kemp, we went everywhere we wanted to go and went in the front door. We was served just like everybody else. In that little old town my daddy was a very prominent man. We never went in the back nowhere, and I just didn't know what segregation was until I came to Dallas. When I first came to Dallas, people said, "You can't go in this place, and you can't go in that place." And I just couldn't understand it.

TINY HAWKINS:
You "niggers" get up and go to the back

One day in 1939 I went with my oldest sister, Emma Jean, to this big red building downtown, the old Dallas County Courthouse. She was getting her divorce from her husband,

and we set down about middle ways in the courtroom. As soon as we sat down, the judge said, "You 'niggers' get up and get to the back." And when he said that, I jumped up and moved to the front. My sister caught ahold to me and was pulling me back. By that time her lawyer came in, and both of them was pulling me, and I drug both of them up to the bar.

I called that judge all kinds of everything you could think of in the book. I told him he wasn't fit to sit behind the bar. The lawyer warned me they have the jailhouse on the next floor. I told him I didn't care. I said, "They made it for people, they didn't make it for cows and horses. So they can just take me there because I don't care, I'm willing to die right now." And I told them if they turned my hand I'd choke 'em to death with my bare hands.

But the judge didn't open his mouth. And they finally got me calmed down and to the back of the courtroom. And when the judge got ready to grant her divorce, we went up, and I just cut him to pieces with my eyes. But they didn't fine me. At that time I could have been tarred and feathered and drug down the street. Dallas was known to be pretty bad with that kind of stuff.

TINY HAWKINS:
I was working for Sam's mother in her beauty salon

During World War II, Sam Hawkins was in the service. I was a beautician, and my friend, Louise, was a barber in the same building. We were writing a lot of soldiers just for the fun, so they would have some letters comin' in. We both was writing Sam only 'cause his mother, our boss, had asked us to.

When Sam would write us back, we'd read each other's letters. And then we would write him again. We'd been writing him approximately six months before he came home on a furlough. We had a 20-dollar bet — which one he was goin' take out. His mother was holdin' the money. She had my 20, and she had Louise's 20. When I saw him, I said, "Oh, Lord, I don't want to go out with him. I don't mind losing the 20 dollars."

Louise had the opportunity of shaving him, massaging him, and giving him a manicure, 'cause she was the barber. But I was setting on the stool doing hair. I found out later he said he didn't see nothin' but my legs, but after he saw my legs, he knew I was the one that he wanted to go out with.

TINY HAWKINS:
Sam was very persistent

Louise and I went out with him together, 'cause we wouldn't go by ourselves. When he

Sam and I got married while he was in the service, right in the middle of World War II.
I loved my husband with all my heart.
We were married 32 years.

*He just wouldn't leave me alone.
He just talked me into it. I married him
so he would stop bugging me.*

went back to his base, he just kept writing, and his writing got a little less with Louise than it did with me. And I was tryin' to make it more with Louise than me, 'cause I really wasn't interested, to tell you the truth. But that was how we met, through the letters. He was a staff sergeant stationed at Ft. Leonard Wood, Missouri.

After he met me, he came down to Dallas every weekend. He was persistent, and after a period of time, we started to date and go out and eventually got married. He just wouldn't leave me alone. He just talked me into it. I married him so he would stop bugging me.

Sam had been born in Dallas. He was actually almost 12 years older than me, and he would tease me often about being his "little country girl." I would come back and say, "Well, Sam Hawkins, you so old that when you was born, Dallas was still in the country!"

We married while he was in the service during the middle of World War II. He got out when our oldest child Charlotte was a month old. That was in 1945, the year the war ended. He served almost six years.

ANN NELSON: (Tiny's younger sister)
When I came to Dallas

When I came to Dallas, we all lived next door to each other. It was Uncle Sam (I called him "Uncle" even though he was my brother-in-law because he was so much older) and Tiny in one house, and me and Ethel and Tom, our brother, in the other. We lived in two houses at 1222 Floride and 1224 Floride.

EVELYN DILLWORTH: (Tiny's older sister)
It's just been
a close-knitted family

It's just been a close-knitted family. Wherever one moved, this is the blessed truth, one of the sisters or the brothers would buy a house next door.

I know two places we lived, we could actually jump off of one porch and onto the other's porch, never even hit the ground, just bounce off.

I had one girl every two years, just like my mama did.
Mama had all of us two years apart. In eight years, I had four girls.
And then I had two sons. I was 23 when I had the first child
and 43 when I had the last.
After I had the first one, my husband said he wanted six.

CHAPTER FIVE

MY HUSBAND SAID HE WANTED SIX KIDS

We had a good time growing up.
The Cinderella Drive-in was one of my favorite places to go on weekends.
Mother would make hot dogs and pop us popcorn.
Yvonne Hawkins Hervey

TINY HAWKINS:
I really hadn't wanted any children

I never wanted any children 'cause I never wanted to see them suffer, and I had taken care of lots of kids in my life. I had seen my brother suffer with asthma, and I didn't want to bring any children in the world and watch them suffer the way he suffered. I had tended to my little nieces and nephews in Kemp, and after I came to Dallas, I tended to white folks' kids.

I had one girl every two years, just like my mama did. Mama had all of us two years apart. In eight years, I had four girls. And then I had two sons. I was 23 when I had the first one and 43 when I had the last.

After I had my first child, Charlotte, my husband said he wanted six. I said, "Oh, well, I don't guess two would be too many." And then I had the next one, and it was a girl, and he wanted a boy so bad. He was a very good daddy. I said, "Well, I guess it wouldn't hurt." We had the third one. Now, the fourth one, we accidentally got her. The fifth and the sixth ones were accidental, too. Didn't want any children, so I compromised on six. I ended up having more than any of my sisters or brothers. I'm the only one that had six. I just didn't want no kids, but I wouldn't take a million dollars for 'em.

TINY HAWKINS:
Butch was supposed to have been a boy

Sam was going to send me back to school when we married, but after I had that first baby, that was the end of going to school. We both was such a nut about our kids until I didn't want to leave them with anybody, and he didn't want me to leave them with anybody. We didn't think nobody could take care of them the way I did.

Butch, my first girl, was Butch before she was born. When I was pregnant, my husband kept saying, "When my son Butch get here, we going to do this, we going to do that," and he just rattled on. Butch was supposed to have been a boy. We named her Charlotte.

Even after nine months, my husband never changed--he kept calling her Butch. And everybody else continued to call her Butch. She wore that name until the day she died.

Then he looked at Sandra after she was born and he said, "My God, this baby looks like me! She's a chip off the old block." So she got the name Chip. And Juliette was so fat until everybody said, "Oh, Peter, Peter, Pumpkin Eater. What a fat baby. She's a pumpkin." So she acquired the name Punkin.

Yvonne, my fourth girl, we never did settle on a name for her. They called her Tweety Bird and called her Red because she was real, real fair. They said she looks like that little old yellow Tweety Bird. Then they called her Penny, but nothing ever stuck but Yvonne. Her Grandfather Hawkins called her Ay-Von.

TINY HAWKINS:
You keep these kids too clean

I was the biggest fool about my kids. I didn't leave them with nobody. Mama always said, "Yeah, you wanted them, you just didn't know you wanted them. Because you're the best mother. As a matter of fact you're the biggest fool mother I ever seen in my life."

Nobody couldn't touch my kids. I had to mop the floors, put newspaper on the floor, then put a quilt on the floor, and then put a sheet on top of the quilt before I let them crawl around.

I was always going to the Dallas clinic. I couldn't afford to go anywhere else. One of the doctors there told me, "You keep these kids too clean. They don't have any ear wax in their ears, and that's the reason why they always have ear infections. Let them get a little dirt on them. They too clean!" This doctor told the other doctors, "She keeps her babies too clean. That's why they always got an ear infection."

I said to him, "Not the way I hear you all

Charlotte knew what everyone should do, and told them.

talking about these nasty babies comin' in here and telling the other mothers to clean their babies up before you all will examine them. You'll never get to say that about one of mine. I haven't never had very much but I was taught to be clean." If my kids ever got any dirt on them, they got it washed off real quick. I had some clean babies, I really did. I was a good wife, mother, Christian.

TINY HAWKINS:
My husband was very protective

He was one of those old-fashioned men that didn't think women were supposed to work. But I said it was the three "W's," "Want, Wait or Work." I had to wait on him to give it to me, or I would want it, or I'd go to work and get it. My attitude was, "I dare you to tell me I can't do it. I'll show you I can."

He just wanted me to stay home and take care of them babies. He was a good provider off of what he made. I had no problems with that. It was just that he couldn't give me all of what

I wanted. And that was one of those three "W's". I wanted a little bit more. It wasn't easy raising a bunch of kids. He was a hard-working man, but black men didn't make much money, and so I had to work. I wanted things for my kids. I didn't want them to go without. And they didn't. I wanted all four girls to have what one girl had. So I worked.

I did the music teacher's hair in exchange for music lessons for my kids. I did the dressmaker's hair in exchange for her sewing. Whatever the needs were, I swapped out with doing hair. And this is what I did.

TINY HAWKINS:

Oh, Lord, when I think about how hard I worked

I always worked because I wanted my own money. I didn't like asking anybody for anything, and I worked at home for years doing hair. I'd take care of my family first, get my kids off to school, get everything done, and then I would have people to come to my house, and I'd do their hair. In the evenings after I cooked dinner, fed my family, got them out of the way, I did hair at night. Sometimes I'd be washing and hanging up clothes at 12:00, one o'clock at night after I put my kids to bed.

SANDRA HAWKINS BRODEN:
(Tiny's second daughter)

There'd be so many women waiting in the kitchen

Mother did all the hair in South Dallas at one point. There'd be so many women waiting in the front of the house trying to get their hair done, she finally had to start making appointments. She did that for many years. On Sundays she'd go to church and see all her handiwork.

SANDRA HAWKINS BRODEN:
(Tiny's second daughter)

We spent lots of time with our aunts

Aunt Ethel's house is very, very nice, very, very clean. It's sparkling all the time. Aunt Ann's the same way. Mama did basic care of our hair, but on a day-to-day basis, Aunt Ann did our hair, she braided it. She dressed us up, she thought we were cute. She had a husband, and she took on us little girls. She did a bunch of things for us.

We grew up at 3908 Atlanta, right around the corner from the nursing home which Mother eventually bought. Our old house has been completely remodeled, and Mother got it rented out now.

We were only allowed to go across the driveway and in our front yard and our backyard. We had a swing in our backyard like they have at parks, not a little bitty red one, I'm talking about the real thing.

My mother's and my aunt's back yards joined together. They were not separated by a fence, so we could go clean across. We had a huge back yard, which was really two back yards.

Daddy used to buy these sacks of oranges and apples, and we used to take bites off of them and throw the rest out the back door. Once when Daddy came home and found them, he told me, "I'm going to show you some kids who don't have nothing, and they'd be glad to have those apples and oranges you're biting off of and throwing out the back door." He took me to West Dallas and showed me some kids that didn't have any shoes.

After that, I stopped wasting food.

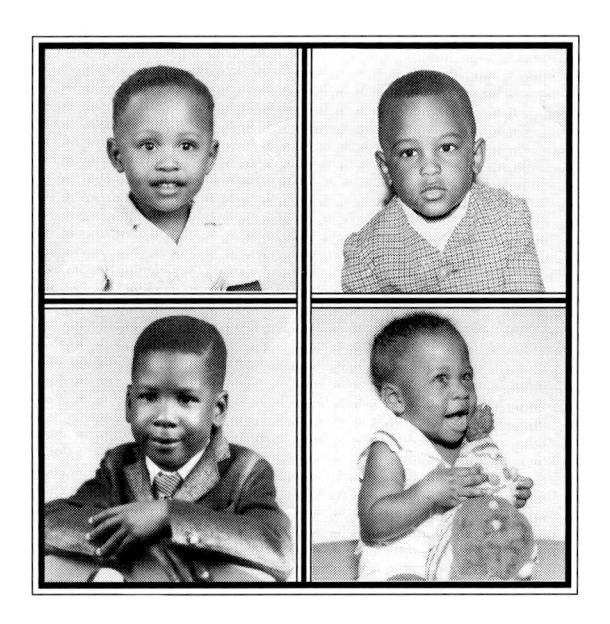

JULIETTE HAWKINS WESLEY: (Tiny's third daughter)
You had to be in yelling distance of Mama in South Dallas

To me, our neighborhood in South Dallas was two or three blocks long, because you had to be in yelling distance of Mama. She had to be able to put her hand on you. She could stand on the front porch and yell down the street and tell us to come home from the park or the store.

The neighborhood was only as far as I could walk, and that wasn't very far. We could walk to the church. But if we had to go to a bible school not in the neighborhood, Mama put us in the car and took us.

There were black-owned stores in the neighborhood, a cab stand and a barber shop, a beauty shop, Miss Simmons' ice cream parlor, A&B Grocery. Dr. Davis Jones, the dentist. Drs. Shelton, Conrad, and Jones, Drs. Dorsey and Page. Dr. Powell. Asher Silberstein, an elementary school, was later changed to Charles Rice when it became a school for black children.

We knew people who lived six or eight blocks away on Latimer, on Eugene, across Pine and Carpenter, and even as far as Southland. That larger area was our community.

JULIETTE HAWKINS WESLEY: (Tiny's third daughter)
Segregation and racism

The first time I remember segregation was at the Dallas Zoo. My Grandfather Hawkins used to visit on Sundays and take us to the zoo in the afternoon. Once, when I was about seven or eight, we had been standing in line waiting to ride some ride, and every time the ride emptied, another group of white kids would get on.

The kids would be making gestures to us like, "You can't get on right now, you won't get on. You stay here, you have to wait." My granddad said, "Y'all will get to ride in just a little bit." We had to stand there such a long time and wait.

Eventually, all us black kids got to get on the ride, but only after the white kids were finished and didn't want to ride anymore. That was the first time I remember segregation.

Then one time when I was about ten, we were shopping at Sears on Lamar. I remember a little white girl calling me a name. The clothes were hanging on a round rack. I just chased her around the rack, grabbed her and whipped her butt and told her if she told anybody, I'd find her, and she'd never tell anything else.

She needed a whipping and I gave it to her. She'll probably have a plug in her head for a long time because I grabbed her by the hair and tried to snatch it out of her. Then I got up and straightened my clothes and came out. I never told my mama because she would have whipped me for doing it.

YVONNE HAWKINS HERVEY: (Tiny's fourth daughter)
I was the baby girl

Growing up being the baby like I was is the biggest thing. I was the baby girl, and I've always been a mother's child. I didn't favor my daddy too much. I was the baby, and I told everything that went on in the house. If they wanted to know something, they could come straight to Yvonne, because I would tell on all my sisters. I was always the one got away with a whole lot because I had older sisters.

Mother was always the go-between between us and Daddy. If we wanted to do something, we always went to her, 'cause he would always say "No."

YVONNE HAWKINS HERVEY: (Tiny's fourth daughter)
I slept with my parents until I was 12

I was afraid when I was a kid. At that time, there were us four girls and Burt. The two older girls had a room, and we two younger girls had a room, and Burt, who was six years younger than me, slept in the baby bed. At first, we girls had two double beds, and we slept together. So after awhile, we got twin beds, and I didn't like sleeping alone.

I would crawl between my mom and daddy from the foot of the bed all the way up. My daddy would wake up and say, "Tiny, this gal's in bed with us." I slept with them until I was 12 years old; then my daddy kicked me out, and I ended up with my brother, little Rod. I slept with him after Mom and Dad put me out.

We used to have family outings. Mother always told us that if we went out in a public place, we'd see water fountains that would have "white" and "colored" on them. She would

Grandmother always said if a thing needs doing, just get on and do it.

always tell us that they were dirty, and she'd have a thermos for us. She said, "You don't want to drink out of that, we got water for you to drink."

If we went somewhere, my mother always had everything we needed. We didn't have to ask for anything or be without anything. It was a close-knit family. My mother wouldn't go in Sanger's or A. Harris because they'd make her put a paper on her head before she could try on hats. At that time, black people could not try on clothes in department stores.

When we were growing up, she would always tell us that we were "just as good as any little white girl" and to "hold your head up right and walk straight." I can remember going to church. The four of us girls walking in a straight line with our dresses flared out. I'm 44 now, so I wasn't old enough to really understand what prejudice was, but my parents always told us that we could do anything that we wanted to do.

We had a good time growing up. The Cinderella Drive-in was one of my favorite places to go on weekends. Mother would make hot dogs and pop us popcorn. We'd take a blanket and get out in front of the car, and Daddy would let us crawl on top of the car.

I think I was about 14 when my mother got pregnant with my baby brother Rodney. We just thought that was the most horrible thing in the world for Mother to be having a baby. We were embarrassed. And the other kids teased me, "Oh, your mother's going to have a baby." She was always active in the PTA, and so when it was time for her to come to my school, I asked her, "Please don't take your coat off." She said, "Why? Are you ashamed of me, Yvonne?" I said, "Mama, it just don't look right." She would keep her coat on for awhile, then she took it off.

My mother has always been my biggest friend. All through my teenage years, she was always there for me. I could tell her anything. She would always come sit on our beds, and if we had problems with the boys or with school, Mother was always there to guide us through it.

SAMUEL BURT HAWKINS: (Tiny's older son)
We had to be in at dark

My father was the disciplinarian of the family. If you messed up, you could expect my daddy was going to take care of you. I can remember I was trying out for St. Phillips football team. Try-outs went past eight or nine o'clock in the evening.

My dad come up there, pulled me out of line, and said, "I told you to be home before sundown." I said, "Dad, I'm trying out." He said, "No, you come home when I say come home. If you had of told me that that's what you were going to do, I'd have been there to see that you got home all right. But you didn't tell me so

you forfeit all that." Our neighborhood was not a place where kids could be safe after dark.

We had to be in at dark. One of Mama's quotes was, "If the sun catch you, if the sun goes down on you, and you outside the house, then you got to pay when you get back in." And she made us pay. We got a spanking, or we had to stay in the next day if the sun went down on you, and you were outside.

When we were growing up, Mama would always tell us that we were "just as good as any little white girl" and to "hold your head up right and walk straight."

SAMUEL BURT HAWKINS: (Tiny's older son)
I have a whole lot of fond memories

Because I had only sisters and before Rodney was born, Dad and I were close. He basically molded me. He would say, "You come with me. You don't need to be around here with all these girls." He had different jobs — a school crossing guard, landscaping, and a truck driver.

In the summertime when he'd go to work in the morning, he'd pick the truck up. At different times he worked delivering oil here in the city for A. H. Jacobs, Ashland Oil Company, Valvoline Oil. He'd bring the truck back around to the house, and I'd go around on his routes with him. On Saturdays, he'd take me to the movies and go pay bills, or whatever he had to do. We had a real good time together.

SAMUEL BURT HAWKINS: (Tiny's older son)
Chunk the snakes to the other side

We could just run berserk all summer long out in the country visiting my grandmother, Willie Mathis, in Kemp. Those were some good times. All my cousins, Baron, Terry, Richard, we'd be down there in the summertime. There was a big old field across from the house and one next to the house. We just could go anywhere then. We'd fish, we'd swim, we'd go huntin', and Granny would just sit out on the porch, and she'd let us do whatever we wanted.

My uncles would take us out, teach us how to shoot and hunt and fish. Those were some good times. Uncle Robert Lee's wife, Ora Lee Mathis, stayed next door to Emma Jean, and Emma Jean stayed next door to Granny. On down the road around the corner lived Aunt Arelia and lots of other relatives. Why, you could go for about five or six miles, and you'd have cousins or your aunts all around you.

My sisters didn't like it down there because we slept out on the porch, even though it was our choice. My answer is, "Oh, shoot, that was fun." There was a lot of cattle ponds. If you chunk the snakes to the other side, you could swim. Like you throw rocks in the pool, and if snakes come up, then you chunk them over to the other side, and then you go swimming.

You wouldn't go real far out because of the sink holes, but you'd go far out enough where you could get wet and splash around. We were young, and that's what they told us to do — before you get in, you chunk those snakes.

SAMUEL BURT HAWKINS: (Tiny's older son)
Our daddy was a character

My sisters have some vivid stories about him because they tell me all the time how they couldn't take boys home because Dad would be sitting in the living room in his underwear cleaning his guns. They said he used to really, really embarrass them.

All my brother-in-laws feared him, I don't know why. They were good friends, and he liked all of them. They all had a real, real good relationship. I guess as far as in-laws go, my mother and father were ideal. They didn't jump in your business, they didn't even ask questions.

We had a basketball goal in the back of the house, and we'd play out there. Mama would come out and play with us. I'd say to her, "Mother, I don't know too many other mamas that's your age can come out here and jump around with us. You're not making the best shots, but you're out here, shooting baskets."

My father gave me the discipline to do things, but my mother gave me a side so that I feel for people. When I was in the service, she would always try to give me advice. If I would get upset, I'd call home, and she would say, "When you got your hand in the lion's mouth, you work easy until you get it out. No, you really don't want to show your hand."

If Mother needs something, she will call me, even though I got a sister who lives nearer to her. She'll call me, and I'll have to drive from DeSoto to run some errand. And I'll get up, go and do it. Me and my brother Rodney, we learned a long time ago that when she calls, just go on and go do whatever it is she wants.

SAMUEL BURT HAWKINS: (Tiny's older son)
My daddy liked Chevys

We had fun, too. We'd go to the drive-in movie on Lamar Street, the King and Star. Every Friday night, Mother fixed sandwiches. We packed into the car, gobbled our food, ran around the drive-in. We had a light blue and white, two-toned Chevrolet Impala. Then we had a green one. My dad liked Chevrolets.

After Rod was born and coming up in the neighborhood, people would say, "Oh, oh, that's Burt's little brother--don't mess with him." Because they knew that would make me mad if you messed with my brother. Me and Rod are real close.

RODNEY HAWKINS: (Tiny's younger son)
Dad and me

When I was six or seven, my mother, Burt, me and my father all drove across country on a trip to California. We stopped at the Grand Canyon. I was overwhelmed at the sight and said, "Geez, look at this." My dad said, "Well, don't you know that I dug this with a teaspoon?" And he pulled out this old beat-up teaspoon and said, "This is the teaspoon that I dug it with right here." And you know, I believed that story up until I got old enough to know better.

He used to tell us all kinds of stories. He had a big round gut. I'd say, "Daddy, why your stomach so big?" And he'd say, "Well, that's because when I was young, I got hungry, and I swallowed a pig whole. And it's still in there right now." And that stomach of his would jump, he'd scare us. He was really, really, really a character. He had some wild tales. He dug the Grand Canyon. He built the Panama Canal by himself with a tractor.

My father passed when I was ten; I was the youngest. There was only me, Mother, and my brother Burt living together for about a year. He's eight years older than me. Then he went off to the service. And from that time until I was 18, there was nobody in the house but me and her.

Mother made sure I was up for school and got me out on time every day. She worked every day, and after work, she cooked and cleaned. She was both mother and father to me until I went in the Navy. I was there five years on a guided missile cruiser.

MORRIS BRODEN: (Tiny's son-in-law and a minister)
Those Hawkins women like hard-working men

My baby kids called Sam "Paw-Paw." I called him "Paw-Paw," too. I looked at my wife's family as being a close-knitted family. Sam loved his family, he loved his children. They were always there for the other. He set a good example for the girls. They say that girls pick a man that's like their dad. He was a hard-working man. I know I'm a hard-working man, too. I guess Sandra saw that in me.

Dr. Hawkins is the type of person who never gets in our business. Matter of fact, if I had a problem, she would always side with me before she would my wife, Sandra. She wouldn't say nothing unless you asked her. Tiny's provided a lot of financial support to all the family, including her sisters, her children, all of them. She's a Christian lady, she is. She's always willing to help, however she could. She has a lot of respect for people. She's a lover of people. You have to be to have a nursing home.

SAMUEL BURT HAWKINS: (Tiny's older son)
My dad and I had a real close relationship.

I can remember the day I left going to the Army. We got up about five o'clock that morning. Dad drove me down to the Union Pacific Train Station and said, "Now you're a man. Take care of yourself. I'll take care of this back here." That was just before he got sick and died.

I stayed in the army two-and-one-half years. I stayed home about six months and then joined the Navy. When I finished basic training the second time, I came back home on leave. When I got home and saw Dad, he didn't even look the same. My dad had been a big man. I mean he could take a barrel full of oil, tip it over, grab it at the bottom, and pick it up and put it on a truck.

When I saw him, he was just a fraction of what he was. That hurt me. He said, "Well, Sam, I told them not to tell you 'cause I didn't want you to worry because you had enough to take care of." My father was real instrumental into what I am right now.

When he was living, Mother called him her backbone. I just do what Mother wants me to do for her like my father did. All the things that I do now, he could do. When I'm mad, my mother calls me, "Sam Hawkins. You're just like your daddy."

Samuel and Tiny Hawkins

TINY HAWKINS:
I couldn't tell you what a loaf of bread cost

I never even went to the grocery store when my husband was alive. He had done all the shopping. I remember he had been dead three months before I went to the grocery store.

Charlotte took me. The bill was $57, and when I got up to the counter, I didn't even have a quarter, didn't have a checkbook, and no money.

Charlotte had to pay for the groceries. I had never had to buy groceries. But I learned to do that, along with all the other responsibilities I had, running the nursing home and seeing after my family.

Fortunately, my children never had to ride the bus.
We had a car, and when they had to go a little bit farther
than they were supposed to, I'd take them to school.
I was at the school so much until they really thought I was a teacher.
Everything that went on, I had to know.

CHAPTER SIX

I DIDN'T HOLD NO LONG MEETINGS

*I was at the school so much
until they really thought I was a teacher. Everything
that went on, I had to know.*
Tiny Hawkins

TINY HAWKINS:

**I organized carpools
to make sure I got my quorum**

Before I became full time at the nursing home, I was a substitute teacher at L.G. Pinkston High. I subbed in math and cosmetology, and I worked in the library and in the office.

My four girls graduated from Lincoln, but the two younger boys, one of them went to David F. Carter, and the other one went to Kimball. Lincoln is a magnet school now. It's on Hatcher and Oakland, about eight or ten blocks from here. They have a beautiful facility.

When I was elected president of the Lincoln High PTA back in the 1960s, we had only about six or seven teachers and 12 to 15 parents coming to meetings. They'd struggle in all times from 7:30 to 8:00 to 8:30 pm.

I asked them, "What day do you want your meeting, and what time do you want your meeting?" They set the time at 7:30, so that's when I'd call the meeting to order. Four of my friends, Ruby Borden, Helen Wortham, Clarice Hawkins, Laverne Harris, and I got in our cars and each went and picked up five people, so I had my quorum. If you were there, and you were interested, we had our meeting. When I left Lincoln as president of the PTA, so many parents and teachers had started coming, often as many as 100, we had to meet in the auditorium.

If anybody came at 8:00, I didn't back up. They started coming on time, because they found out I wasn't going to repeat what I had said. If they came in as late as 8:30, we'd already be through with our business, we were leaving.

Since I worked at home doing hair, I usually had some free time during the day to make phone calls. Here's what I did. I didn't wait for anybody to come. I got on the phone and had my people ready on time. I kept to the schedule and told them what was what, and we faced whatever issues needed to be faced. We worked with the principal, we got things done. We had parents with kids in band and ROTC, and we got involved in everything.

I was always down at the school board meetings whenever there was something wrong.

I went down to complain about those portable buildings where the kids had to transfer from the main building out to the portables. I gathered me up a unit of people, and we went down to see to it that they do something better than those portables.

We accomplished our little goals. This was at Charles Rice elementary school right near here, what used to be Silberstein School near Poplar and Pine.

We did work out a solution so the kids wouldn't have to be out in the rain going from place to place. I think they transferred some students from one school to the other, and that eliminated the over-crowdedness. Other students were assigned to Pearl C. Anderson and to John Henry Brown, according to what neighborhood they lived in.

Fortunately, my children never had to ride the bus. We had a car, and when they had to go a little bit farther than they were supposed to, I'd take them to school.

I was at the school so much until they really thought I was a teacher. Everything that went on, I had to know. Like who was teaching my kids, what kind of background they had, where they came from, and what they were teaching them. I just didn't want any and everybody teaching my kids. Most of my kids' teachers — if we had one run-in, we didn't have another one, because we became good friends.

The teachers found out that I was really interested in my children's education and their well-being. So I really didn't have a problem. And the teachers would let me know if my kids didn't do what they were supposed to, 'cause I was for the right thing.

I'm the youngest.

TINY HAWKINS:
I don't know how I got all those kids in the car

I carried my kids to the football games, and I'd go back and pick them up, or one of the other parents would take them and I'd pick them up. We'd carpool. I'd have mine and a half dozen of somebody else's. I had to take one child one place and one that place and one another place. By the time I got through dropping them all off, it was time to start picking them up. I never did go to the games unless it was a really big one.

YVONNE HAWKINS HERVEY: (Tiny's fourth daughter)
We were always taught to protect ourself

I only got in trouble one time in my life, and that was my senior year in high school. I was dating a football player, and I had his jacket on one day in school. Two girls, his cousin and her friend, were out to get me.

I walked through the door into class, put my jacket on my chair, and one of them knocked it off. I picked the jacket up, went to my seat, put my books down, and I came back. We just had some little girl conversations and oh, we got into a fight. I took my shoe off and popped one of the girls in the head.

Then I went into the bathroom and washed my shoe off, I washed all the blood off my shoe, I washed my hands up, and I went to the office, and I was just sitting there. Then the principal's voice came over the PA system, "Find the other girl." (That was me!) They couldn't figure out who this other girl was that just did all this fighting. They was looking for the other girl, and I was so afraid.

I never will forget this. The principal said, "Hawkins, what are you doing in here?" I say, "I'm the other girl you're looking for." And he said, "WHAT? You better call Tiny."

The principal knew my mother. Everybody knew my mother since she was the PTA president. So I got on the phone and called my mother at the nursing home. I said, "Mother, I'm in trouble." She said, "What have you done?" I said, "I had a fight." She said, "Are you hurt?" I said, "No, but the other girl is." She said, "Well, I'll be there in ten minutes."

So the other girl's mom came up to the office, and met my mom.

My mother's trying to be nice. She said, "I'm so sorry that the two girls got into a fight. I'm willing to pay for any damages. You can take your daughter to any hospital that you want to and get her stitched up."

This lady was carrying on, saying what she was going to do to my mama, so my mama stood up and said, "Now, look. My daughter done beat the hell out of your daughter, and if you don't shut up, you going to get the same thing." And I was so surprised! My mother's just calm as can be. The principal said, "Okay, Tiny, I'll take care of this. Just take Yvonne home and bring her back tomorrow."

In this case, I didn't do the first hitting, the other girl hit me. I said, "Mama, I didn't pick no fight, it was two of them, and they were picking at me."

I went home. It was right before graduation, and I just knew I was going to get expelled and wasn't going to get to walk across the stage. But it worked out okay. I didn't get suspended, and I went back to school. My parents did punish me. I didn't get to participate in the senior activities like the senior picnic. That was the only punishment. It wasn't a real serious punishment because I had never had a fight in school before.

My mother told us to always protect ourselves, so I didn't start it, but she would always tell us to "finish it," and I did.

It took me 15 years of going to school at night
to get my bachelor's degree.
I just kept taking courses and getting credits and
before I knew it,
I was working on a Ph.D. in
Vienna, Austria, in a place built back in the 1400s.

CHAPTER SEVEN

I WAS LIKE A RABBIT IN A BRIAR PATCH

*What made me stay on at the nursing home
was a lot of people who said they needed me.
So I stayed not for the money, but for the need.*
Tiny Hawkins

TINY HAWKINS:
I first started here in 1967

The South Dallas Nursing Home was the first nursing home I had ever been in in my life, didn't even know what one was. I was recruited by the director of social services who needed an activity director. She had tried out three or four, but nobody came up to what she expected.

Here's how she found me. She was a little depressed, so she just got in her car and drove around in my neighborhood. When she saw a car on the Salem Baptist Church parking lot, she got out and went in and talked to the minister and gave him a description of the kind of person she would love to have for an activity director.

She wanted to know whether or not his wife or anybody in his church would be interested. He told her that the description didn't fit his wife or anyone in the church, "But I do know a lady like the one you are describing. I don't know what she does, but I'll give you her pastor's name, and you can call him." She called my pastor and got my telephone number, and then she called me.

TINY HAWKINS:
I guess it was God-sent

I guess they bugged me for about three months before I came over here to work. After they described the job, I told them that sounded like the same kind of work I'd been doing free of charge anyway for 20 years. So I took the job. I guess it was God-sent. I guess that's the way He was directing my path.

I told them they could give me two dollars a day to cover my gas expense because I was living near here on Atlanta. And I set my own hours. I came in when I wanted to come, and I left when I wanted to leave.

I said, "I'll work three days a week--Monday, Tuesday, Wednesday." Thursday, Friday, and Saturday, I planned to continue doing hair because I could make good money, 50 dollars easy as a beautician. When I got my first pay check, I was surprised at what they paid me. They ended up paying me 20 dollars a day.

But the money at the nursing home wasn't something that really made me remain. I became

The nursing home has never been about money for me. I made more money cutting hair in my kitchen.

close to one little white patient who had no family. I'd come and smoke a cigarette with her, and one Wednesday when I told her I wouldn't see her until Monday, she began crying, "The days are so long without you."

TINY HAWKINS:
I stayed for the need

And there was more. Some of the residents didn't know their rights under Medicare and Medicaid. Some staff didn't take the time to see to it that their needs was met. There's a lot of things that's offered, but if you don't know how to get 'em, then you end up without 'em.

In the meantime, administration was trying to get me to stay anyway, and I wasn't making but 17 dollars a day as a substitute teacher. So I decided to stay here and not go back to the school system. The nursing home raised my salary more than what I was making in the school system, but that didn't make me stay.

What made me stay on was a lot of other people who said they needed me. So I stayed not for the money, but for the need. Because I have never had any money, and I wouldn't know what to do with it if I had it, 'cause if I had it, I'd give it away, or I'd put it back in the business, or I'd do something for somebody with it. So that's how I ended up being here.

When I first started as activity director, I would read to the residents. We had arts and crafts, we made pottery, we made baskets. If there was anything that I didn't know how to do, I got me a book, and I learned on my own. Then a lady came in and showed me how to make pottery on our kiln. And me and the patients learned together.

TINY HAWKINS:
I learned from looking over peoples' shoulders

And then I sneaked off at night and went to school about the third week I was here to learn about the nursing home business. All those white folks with degrees working here thought I knew more than what I knew. I went out to El Centro, didn't tell anybody. I went to Blue Cross/Blue Shield to learn the Medicare-Medicaid program. Soon I knew it better than the other staff did.

TINY HAWKINS:
I just cut all a-loose

At that time I was the only black professional here on the administrative staff. I stayed activity director about four, five months, and then the chief administrator moved me to social services. I did have some educational background in social work. I took care of the residents' social needs.

And that was just like puttin' a rabbit in a

briar patch. I just cut all a-loose. I was out in the community, I was doing everything, I was really getting these folks set up and giving them what they needed then.

If they didn't know how to do something, I found out how you do it, and I got it done.

TINY HAWKINS:
I had a mind of my own

The first raise I got after I was transferred to social services was because I refused to do what the social director told me to do. She said for me to do a certain thing, and I told her, "That's not the way you do it." I knew that what she was telling me to do was wrong, because I had originally gone to Blue Cross and Blue Shield, and I had already got some information from the Department of Human Services.

So I said, "No, Patricia, I'm not goin' to do that. If you want that done, you're the director, you do it." The dispute was about some patients' files and money, the way they were appropriated, what you was supposed to do, and what you was not supposed to do.

It was pretty serious. And we could have had some extra money coming into the facility if I had done it her way, but I knew that she was wrong. If it was found out, the money would have been taken back, and the nursing home could have been charged with fraud. That's the reason I told her I wasn't goin' to do it.

So she reported me to the assistant administrator, and he called me in. He said, "Tiny, why didn't you do what Patricia told you to do?" I said, "Because it isn't right, that's not what you're supposed to do, I'm not going do it." He said, "Yeah, you going to do it."

I said, "Look, I wasn't looking for a job when I came here. You all sent for me. So, I'm not going to do it. I can go home." And he said, "We don't want you to go home, Tiny." I said, "Well, I can, because I'm not going do it." He said, "We better call the chief." I said, "You can call the chief all you want to. It don't make me no difference. I told you I wasn't going to do it, and I'm not going to do it."

TINY HAWKINS:
Tiny, why won't you cooperate?

The assistant administrator called the CEO, the chief in Oklahoma, and he came down the next week. And he met with the five of us in social services. I'm the one that's rocking the boat, even though we were all good friends, too.

The CEO said, "Tiny, I understand that you are creating a problem in this facility. Why won't you cooperate?" I said, "Well, you can eliminate that now, I can go home if I'm the problem. Because I am not going to do what they got set up to do. It's as simple as that." And I got up to go.

The rabbit in the briar patch.

53

I never dreamed I would own
a nursing home when I grew up.

He said, "Wait a minute, wait a minute." So they called a social worker at the Department of Human Services who came out the next afternoon to meet with us. The social worker quoted verbatim what I had told them. So the chief looked at me. They all looked at me. And I just got up and went on to my office.

TINY HAWKINS:
Tiny, we going to give you a raise

Pretty soon the chief came to my office and said, "Tiny, I'm sure glad that you didn't do that, because if you had, next year we sure would have been in a lot of trouble with the federal government. We going to give you a raise." I said, "I sure appreciate it. But a raise is not going to suffice. I want Patricia's job. We're good friends, but I want her job. Because I refuse to work under anybody who is incompetent, and she is to me. I either get her job, or you get my resignation."

So in about three hours, Patricia had been moved to bookkeeping, and I was the director of social services, with a raise. We never lost our friendship. I was the director of social services for less than 18 months, then I was the assistant administrator. And in two years, I was the administrator.

TINY HAWKINS:
The men in the class gave us holy hell

I had a provisional administrator's license. Then it became mandatory that you have a license to be an administrator, and the owner and administrator was a very generous person. He sent about a half a dozen of us to school.

In the beginning, the men thought we were beneath them because we were women. They felt like we women was invading their territory. They were just sarcastic. They gave us holy hell.

They'd say things like, "Women just don't know what they are doin'." "You don't have any business bein' in here." Most of the white women took it, but me and a couple of them, we went to bat with the men. And before it was over with, they were all around us, we were their equals. A lot of them meeting me now at conferences say, "My God, here comes the world's worst."

I graduated from El Centro in 1971 with about 47 others. I was the only black in the class, with about 13 women. I became the 647th person in the State of Texas to be licensed. My license number is 647. And I was the first black in Texas to own and operate a nursing home.

TINY HAWKINS:
**I was always taking one course
or another in something**

Going back to school was something I

always wanted to do and didn't have a opportunity, so whatever became available to me, I just used it to my best advantage. It was just my desire from a kid up. I just felt like an education is something I was supposed to have.

It took me 15 years of going to school at night to get my bachelor's degree. Being a nursing home administrator, you do a lot of continuing education. I just kept taking courses and getting credits and before I knew it, I really was working on a Ph.D. And then it came a time when they said, "You need to do your dissertation." And I just continued to study.

Later, I went to Vienna, Austria, to study and complete the work for my doctoral dissertation. The facility where I studied is the largest in Vienna, built back in the 1400s. It has a nursing home and a hospital associated with it. I received my doctorate in 1988 from Pacific Western University. The title of my dissertation was "Principles of Management in Health-Care Institutions."

This last trip that I took to Turkey was a continuing education tour for nursing home administrators. You get credits for that travel, and the weeks that we spent in Turkey is equivalent to three hours towards a degree.

TINY HAWKINS:
Go to school, go to school, go to school

My sisters and brothers have a good education. I pushed all my kids, my grandkids, everybody that I knew — go to school, go to school, go to school. I just think it's important that you do these things. And I've sent quite a few of my staff to school.

My niece Mattie Helen first came to the nursing home to work as a nurse's aide. I then sent her to El Centro Junior College to get certified as an activity director, a position she has held for 21 years.

My grandson, Mark, started coming to the nursing home as a little boy. Six years ago he began working at the home during summers, and after taking some courses at El Centro, was eventually promoted to activity director. He assists the residents with exercising, walks around the grounds and putting together social events with other homes, such as domino tournaments.

My eldest daughter, Charlotte, came to work here about two years after I did, around 1969. I needed a receptionist and called and asked her did she want to come work over here. She had studied laboratory technology at North Texas State University and started here as a receptionist and lab assistant. I sent her to El Centro to study for her administrator's license and when she graduated, she became the assistant administrator under me. She knew every part of this business. I guess if she were alive today, I could have retired.

Charlotte is seated on the far right.

My daughter that passed, Charlotte, was like me.
You couldn't make her do anything.

CHAPTER EIGHT

LOSING A CHILD IS THE WORST THING

*Charlotte was just the greatest mom on earth.
She was a beautiful person.
She was the sweetest person,
but when you made her mad, go on from there.*
Mark Finley (Charlotte's son)

TINY HAWKINS:

My husband was just crazy about Butch

Sam couldn't wait until his first child, Butch, was born. He knew with all his heart she was going to be a boy. Poor man, he waited through four daughters before he got his first son. Butch came and we named her Charlotte.

I remember when Butch (Charlotte) was born. Sam was stationed in Missouri and had to be called and told that his baby girl was born. Sam arrived at the hospital in the middle of the night in his uniform and was informed visiting hours were over. He raised so much sand that the nurse let him in to see his first born. The baby was in the nursery, and the nursery had told him he could only look at the baby, but that wasn't good enough for Sam.

He started raising a lot more sand, and the nurse finally in desperation brought Butch (who wasn't wearing a diaper) to her Daddy. Butch filled his hand, and not with urine. Sam, not to be outdone, put the baby in his arms, and wiped his hands clean on the front of that nurse's uniform. I remember that night so well because

he then insisted on coming into my room to see me. To avoid another incident, probably because he was an intimidating figure in his uniform in those days of segregation, the nurses complied.

TINY HAWKINS:

Charlotte was like me

My daughter that passed, Charlotte, was like me. You couldn't make her do anything. I found that out very early in her life.

When she was three or four years old, I gave her a whupping and told her to go to bed. I could not make her go to bed, so I just picked her up and threw her in the bed. I knew then that that was me coming out.

I never did that again, because I knew that I would never break her spirit, so I didn't try it anymore.

Charlotte got breast cancer in 1980 and died three years later. With the help of my children, grandchildren, nieces and nephews, I began to deal with my grief. Also, running the nursing home kept my mind on helping others.

SANDRA HAWKINS BRODEN:
(Tiny's second daughter, Charlotte's sister)
I was very close to Charlotte

You would have had to know her. Charlotte was the leader. She'd give Mother word-for-word. Mama would say to her, "You not going to do this." And she would say to Mama, "Yes, I am going to." But not me. I wasn't that brave. Never gave Mama a back word in my life, never talked back or anything.

She was very close to Mama, and I was very close to Butch. Mother will tell you that over the last three or four years, I've become closer to her because I was closer to my sister. Because when I was growing up, Charlotte took care of me.

Nobody messed with Charlotte's sister. We were two years apart in age, but I was smart, I started school when I was five. She finished school one year, I finished the next.

SANDRA HAWKINS BRODEN: (Charlotte's sister)
We'd have our secrets

What I miss most is when she'd call me up, and we'd giggle about something together, two sisters, and we'd have our secrets. We'd laugh a lot, have a lot of fun together. I miss so much the camaraderie, the closeness that we shared. A lot of things I couldn't share with anybody else but her. Some of those things Mama doesn't even know about today.

SANDRA HAWKINS BRODEN: (Charlotte's sister)
I was very angry when she died

Charlotte was basically my sister/mother/mentor. When she died, I said, "Why did you do this to me? Because I cannot be the oldest. You can take it back, I don't want it."

Unlike Charlotte, I've never had an outgoing personality. Believe it or not, I was the shyest person in the world. I never said anything growing up. Whatever Mama said or whatever anybody said, it was okay with me.

A lot of the things, I guess, from example I took up from Charlotte. She used to get so angry with me because I wouldn't speak up for myself. "You just take it. You cannot sit around and do that, you got to stand up."

And I could hear her saying those things, and I still sometimes now hear her saying, "You better not sit there and take that, you better get up and say something." She's been dead awhile now, and I've taken on a lot of those characteristics that she had because I've had to. That coaching and knowing what she would have said.

JULIETTE HAWKINS WESLEY:
(Tiny's third daughter, Charlotte's sister)
And I don't intend to tell anybody twice

Charlotte was always the parent when

Mother was not around. I remember when Daddy died, Charlotte was the take-charge person, the tyrant, the general, chief-in-charge.

When we got to the hospital, Charlotte told us, "There will be no display of uncontrollable behavior because Mother doesn't need that right now. You will walk in there, you will pay your respects to Daddy, you will come out of that room, you will dry your eyes, and you will not break down. And I don't intend to tell anybody that twice. Is that understood?" And I thought, "How can you tell me that I can't cry? This is my daddy, and he's dead."

After I finished crying, she said, "Mother's sitting in the hall, and we're going out there, and she needs to know that you have it together," and that's what we did.

Then Charlotte picked out Daddy's burial clothes, she picked out what Mother was going to wear, she got the insurance papers, she sat down and made out the program — all that was done that day. The next day she got boxes from the store, she packed up all Daddy's clothes, and cleaned the room. And she never entered the house again until she got sick herself.

RODNEY HAWKINS:
(Tiny's younger son, Charlotte's brother)
It was like putting two rams in an arena

Charlotte and Mother, I guess they kind of grew up together in the business. I don't think any of us have that same grasp that Charlotte had. Charlotte and my mother were a lot alike. When they were together, it was like putting two rams in an arena.

They would argue a lot, but the relationship worked. All my sisters and my brother, they

When one is down, the other needs to be there to pick that one up.

say growing up, Charlotte was like their mother. When they were younger, when my mother was working, Charlotte used to whip them and make them clean up. She was like Mom's stand-in.

I actually believe if Charlotte had been living right now, Mother wouldn't be working. Charlotte could run the business, she was the assistant administrator and actually the administrator. She was the only one of us that had actually taken over the business. She was doing everything, she made all the decisions. She had a grasp on everything and every department.

RODNEY HAWKINS: (Charlotte's younger brother)
We got really close when she got sick

I guess of all my sisters Charlotte and I weren't really that close until she got sick. She died of breast cancer. We developed a real, real close relationship in the last year-and-a-half of her life. She was sick at the time, but she had had her surgery, and she was doing all right.

We went to Palm Springs, Mother and her

and me. And Charlotte took me to the bar and bought me a drink, and we talked, and we developed a real close relationship. She came and stayed with Mother and me for the last six months or year of her life, because she couldn't take care of herself. Her cancer had gotten too bad. We were talking every day when I got home from school, having good conversations.

RODNEY HAWKINS: (Charlotte's younger brother)
Her death was really hard on my mom

And the day she died, I had been out of town to the World Jamboree with the Boy Scouts for two weeks. I didn't even know she had gotten worse. She didn't die until I got back and went to the hospital. I talked to her, and about 30 minutes later she passed. My mom said she never thought she would outlive one of her kids. She's said she's lost everything, but that was the hardest thing for her.

Her death was very hard especially on Yvonne because they were real, real close. Wherever Butch (that was Charlotte's nickname) lived, like in an apartment complex, Yvonne lived in the same one. They moved all around together. Then when Butch lived in a particular neighborhood, Yvonne moved to that neighborhood. And Yvonne got all her advice from her and talked to her all the time, so it was real, real hard on her.

MONA FINLEY:
(Tiny's granddaughter, Charlotte's daughter)
She was everything to me

She can't talk for herself, but I can talk for her. She was an outstanding mother, and she was the type of person who didn't let things worry her too much until her health failed, then everything started worrying her. She got to where she just couldn't take it. To me, she didn't feel like she wanted to fight any more.

The fondest time that I can remember is when we used to go to the mall. She liked to window shop. She loved clothes. At the grocery store she'd say, "Put what you want in the basket. You want to eat steaks? Get some steaks." We didn't have to live on a budget. We were able to eat the type of food that we wanted. We had a good life, me and my brother did. We lived comfortably, and when she expired, then all kind of stuff went kaput.

My mother didn't see my oldest son, she didn't see any of my children. I miss that the worst, that she didn't get to see my children, and she's never going to see their children on earth. She'll see them in another life, because I do believe that you will see the person again. I was raised up believing that you will see the dead again. It might not be the body, but the spirit.

She was everything to me. Everything that I did to my mother, my son who is 11 is doing me worse. I started at 13. She said, "When you have children, then you'll understand, and you'll know what I'm talking about, because if you keep doing me like this, your kids are going to do you worse."

I wish I could say, "Mama, you were right." I wish I could go talk to her and tell her everything. She probably knows what I'm going through. Everything that she said, it came true. And I can't get mad at my son. I try to tell him like she tried to tell me, but, honey, you can't.

When she worked here at the nursing home, she was very well liked. Everyone loved her, she was a beautiful person. During the time that she was ill, I caused a lot of problems. I was a wild child. The type of child that you couldn't tell anything. Like Mama.

The older I get, I guess the more I favor my mother. Every time Grandma looks at me, she gets sad. Because my mother was her first-born child, and I'm her first-born grandchild.

I know my grandma loves me, but I've never been like her daughter. Her daughter was something else, she was terrific. Maybe when she look at me, she gets mad because I didn't turn out to be like my mother. She was Charlotte, and I'm Mona.

I can only do what I can do. I can't be something that I'm not. I'm not going to try to do that to make my grandma happy.

MARK FINLEY: (Tiny's grandson, Charlotte's son)
She would always stay on me

She was just the greatest mom on earth. She was a beautiful person. She was the sweetest person, but when you made her mad, go on from there. My nose used to run a lot, and she always said, "Mark, blow your nose." Now, every time my nose runs, everybody says, "Mark, blow your nose." It reminds me of her 'cause she used to stay on me.

If I even coughed, she took me to the doctor 'cause I had asthma a lot. I used to try and hide it from her, but she would always find out, and I had to go to the doctor. I hate doctors even now, I don't like to go.

DON BRODEN: (Tiny's grandson, Charlotte's nephew)
Charlotte was my favorite aunt

She really was; she was my heart. We were both born under the same sign, we were both Scorpios. She was just one of the sweetest ladies. I figured that she always took a shining to me, too. When I was a kid, I asked my mama all the time, "Can I spend the night at Charlotte's?" And summers, too. She was a hell of a lady. I miss her, I miss her. I wonder all the time how would life be if she was here.

WILLIE ARNOLD: (Tiny's grandson, Charlotte's nephew)
My memories of Charlotte are very good memories

She was a very sweet person, but she could also be a hellcat. Push the wrong buttons, and she could be one of your worst enemies. We were very, very close. Almost up until her last days, she was at my grandmother's house. Sometimes when everyone else was gone, I'd go over there and stay.

BURT HAWKINS: (Charlotte's younger brother)
Charlotte and I were real close

I knew she was sick, but she was doing pretty good. Matter of fact, before she died of breast cancer, I was still in California in the Navy. Me and Belinda were married. I had talked to Charlotte on the phone maybe two months before she died, and she said, "Well, Burt, I'm going to start sending you some little funny cards." Then she says if she gets real sick, or if anything happens, she'd call and tell me.

We were off the coast of Managua doing this scrimmage, and I was gone for a couple of months. The Red Cross couldn't get to me. Came back, and when we were pulling into port, my chief petty officer came down and told me, "What you was expecting to happen has happened." Charlotte had already died. I couldn't have got back in time for the funeral anyway, so they waited 'til I got to port to tell me. That really upset me, but that was my last cruise anyway, so I was about ready to get out.

I came on home and said, "Well, I'll stay here now." Charlotte would be the one that would be in Mother's place right now if she had lived. I was older then so I said to myself, "I got a kid on the way, I'm married." I settled down, and here I am now. I already had my nursing home licenses, and I kept them up to date.

JULIETTE HAWKINS WESLEY: (Charlotte's younger sister)
These are binding things

This family has had our share of sadness with cancer. After Charlotte died, I remember when Yvonne, our youngest sister, was in the hospital because she found a big lump in her breast. We were so frightened because Charlotte had had breast cancer.

At first the doctor told Yvonne that nothing was wrong, her mammogram was fine, and her pain was probably from her hormones. She couldn't believe it, went to Parkland and told them she wasn't leaving until she found out what was really wrong with her.

Finally, a doctor found the lump by doing a surgical biopsy. He told us it was the third stage of cancer, and it was so large she wasn't going to live. We refused to accept that. I told him, "You don't know everything, and she will live."

And Yvonne said, "I'm not ready to die. My son Willie doesn't have anybody but me, and I got to make sure that he graduates from high school." She took chemotherapy, had surgery, and then she had radiation. And the tumor went away.

And every year on her birthday, we recognize it, and I say, "There's my baby sister, you made it. You were not supposed to be here anymore, but here you are." There's not a dry eye in the place. And we say, "God is so good."

And He has been good to this family. We've lost a lot, but in losing, we've gained a lot. It binds you to another when you lose someone. These powerful things in your life, those are binding things."

There's my baby sister, Yvonne, with her son, Willie, Jr. You were not supposed to be here, but here you are.

We had to be in at dark. One of Mama's house rules was,
"If the sun catch you,
if the sun goes down on you, and you outside the house,
then you got to pay when you get back in." And she made us pay.
We got a spanking, or we had to stay in the next day if the sun
went down on you, and you were outside.

I have five kids, all my children now,
working here at the nursing home,
plus a sister, two grandkids, one niece, and one great-niece.

Sandra, Yvonne, Juliette
Burt, Tiny, Rodney

CHAPTER NINE

IT'S A FAMILY AFFAIR

*Dr. Hawkins runs the business like a Christian organization.
She treats everybody right.
The residents are her foremost concern,
and she wants them treated with dignity and respect.*
Lily Green (Long-time employee)

TINY HAWKINS:
A place to live, not to die

In the early 1970s, Jack Counts, the owner of the South Dallas Nursing Home, wanted to close it because it was unprofitable and he already had two others.

He asked me to move with him, but my roots were in South Dallas, and I wouldn't leave.

I decided to buy the business from him, and in so doing, began trying to assume the $500,000 mortgage to keep the nursing home in business. The mortgage-holder was skeptical since seven white male administrators before me were unable to make a profit. I had two strikes against me: I was black and a woman.

I said, "Don't compare me with the seven men. I'm not them. I'm a black mama." I made my final mortgage payment in October of 1980.

There had been no other black nursing home administrators in the state before me. Since then I have taught many interns how to be nursing home administrators.

TINY HAWKINS:
It's more than a challenge

I have five kids, all my children, working here at the nursing home, plus a sister, two grandkids, one niece, and one great-niece.

I have lots of relatives working here. I haven't learned how to deal with it yet. It's more than a challenge. You can't ignore that fact.

Sometimes your heart says one thing, and your business sense says another.

I have also taken care of a lot of my relatives during their later years here at the nursing home.

When my mother was no longer able to live alone in Kemp, she stayed with my baby sister Ann for several years until she became ill and had to come to the nursing home. We moved my mother here, and I put her in the room right across the hall from my office, so I could slide my chair over and peep in there and see how she was throughout my shift.

SANDRA HAWKINS BRODEN: (Tiny's second daughter)
All of us are independent

Because I'm the oldest living one of the children, I see in all of us a certain amount of independence. I don't want to be on a pedestal that I'll fall off of.

When Mother isn't there, we can function one way or another. All of us have a little bit of something that she's given us, the ability to make it because all of us are independent.

At this point, every one of us has at one time or another worked for her. When I left Texas and came back, I worked for her only a year. And from that point on, I said, "No, I need to make my own niche," so I went to work for Southwestern Bell for 20 years.

JULIETTE HAWKINS WESLEY: (Tiny's third daughter)
**I'm probably more like her
than any of her children**

I've been here about a year. I actually came here to be the personnel director and in-service coordinator and to serve as Ms. Hawkins' administrative assistant. It has been a greater learning curve than I anticipated. But I did have 25 years of business experience in management in telecommunications. So I think it was the management background she was looking for that I could bring to the table.

I know I have a big job, and some days I pray for a couple of more inches on the shoulders so I can actually stand up to the challenge. I feel a sense of independence. If any of her children were just like her, it probably would be me, because I do take things very seriously. Where she would take care of everything for me, I have to take care of it for myself. But I can't

Here I am signing the papers
to buy the nursing home for a half million dollars.

take care of everything for everybody. My shoulders are not that big.

Mama has the biggest heart and the biggest shoulders of anybody I've ever known. She wants all of us to be ready to stand on their own two feet, just like I want my children to stand on their own two feet.

JULIETTE HAWKINS WESLEY: (Tiny's third daughter)
**Working with family is
the biggest challenge**

That's a positive thing to be surrounded by family. But it offers a different type of technique for taking care of business than I was accustomed to. Fortunately, I am also able to draw the line where business and family come into play.

I'm more like her in being able to balance and be fair, be forthright and honest. Sometimes I have to temper what I say at the nursing home because it's family. When relatives mess up, if it affects the business, then there is no family love, no parent-child relationship — it's business.

But I'm also unlike her in a lot of ways. She's a very big group person, whereas I like intimate things. I'm happy at home with my husband and my kids and Friday night football instead of a banquet and sequins.

RODNEY HAWKINS: (Tiny's younger son)
I was a little terror

I was eight when Mother bought the nursing home. I remember nights when she and Aunt Ann would wake me up, put me in the back seat, and they'd come over here and work.

I really grew up out here, yeah, I did. I was a terror. Ask Joe Langley, the head of maintenance. I used to pull the rails off the wall and take the hammers and beat holes. Joe remembers, "I'd hate to see you coming, because I knew you was going to tear up something. You were so destructive."

Joe never used to tell Mother. He'd fix whatever I'd broken and send me on my way. He'd take me to the store and buy me a pickle and tell me to go sit down and leave things alone.

RODNEY HAWKINS: (Tiny's younger son)
I'm still the baby to everybody

Once in a while I think I'm not going to work here anymore because sometimes your siblings get on your nerves. I'm still the baby to everybody, and they always want to tell me what to do. I have to tell them all the time, "Yeah, I'm a grown man, too, you know, I make my own decisions." But I see myself working here for a long time, I do.

Since Mother's worked all of her life for this, and she's done it for her family and for her children, I think we should stay here and carry on the tradition for our children.

Miss Lily Green, the bookkeeper who's semi-retired, trained me, taught me everything she knows. Most of the patients here are on Medicaid. I do the payroll, accounts payable, accounts receivable. I oversee the departmental budgets, and if the department heads go over their budgets, I let Dr. Hawkins know, and she lets them know.

We got around 80, 81 employees right now [1995]. Last year, we've had 150 off and on the payroll, that's the turnover. It's not a glamorous job, being a nurse's aide. It's hard work, and you have to have a knack for it.

I've worked in every department except nursing services, because I can't deal with that part. Now I can talk with the residents, I enjoy them. But as far as bathing them and cleaning them up, I just can't handle that. Dr. Hawkins always says, "Why don't you come in and make

When Mother came to the nursing home, I put her right across the hall from my office where I could scoot my chair over and check on her.

some beds?" I say, "Well, if it's messy, I don't like seeing the residents down or in a bad way." I guess I'm too soft-hearted.

Over the years I've gotten real close to a lot of residents. It is really, really hard when one of them dies. Some of them have been here a long, long time; they're like members of your family.

Business is business, and family is family.

BURT HAWKINS: (Tiny's younger son)
When you come in the door, she's not "Mother"

Mother comes here almost every day, even on weekends. A lot of times you don't need to actually physically be here. If something happens, they're going to call. She could go home if she wanted to. Another thing, she's got all her kids working here with her, but that doesn't matter. Business is business, and family is family.

When we come in here, she's either "Dr. Hawkins" or "Miss Hawkins," not "Mother." The only way she gets a rest is if she leaves town; that's why she travels so much, so she doesn't feel obligated to come in.

RODNEY HAWKINS: (Tiny's younger son)
The residents always come first to her, no matter what

Generally when Dr. Hawkins first comes in, she rattles the tree, rattles all of us. Then she makes her rounds and talks to all the patients. She knows them all by name. They're all "Sweetheart" and "Darling." "How are you? What's going on? Has anybody been doing anything to you? Well, if they do, just call my name and let me know."

She asks them, "Have you eaten? Have you had any water? " And that's every day, two and three times a day. She checks for the cleanliness of the building.

PORTIA SAMUELS: (Tiny's great-niece)
Mattie Helen is the one that she calls

When Aunt Tiny really needs something done, when she got somebody coming in she want to prepare for and have things laid out and fixed up, Mattie Helen is the one that she calls.

LILY GREEN: (Bookkeeper and Tiny's friend)
Miss Hawkins and I go back a long way

I came to Dallas in 1972, moved here from New Orleans where I had worked for Western Union Telegram with the accounting department. After about a year, I heard from a friend that Dr. Hawkins needed a part-time worker.

So in October 1974, she hired me over the telephone as the bookkeeper. She had just bought the business about three months before, and she stated she was at her lowest point. I told her the only thing she needed was some help, and I knew she could make it. I've been with her ever since. I'm still here, 21 years later.

Many of the other department heads have been here a lot of years--dietary, nursing service, housekeeping, administration, and maintenance. Joe Langley, the maintenance supervisor, has been with her longer than I have. The cook, Letha Berts, has been here a long time, too.

LILY GREEN: (Bookkeeper and Tiny's friend)
Dr. Hawkins is a very determined person

Dr. Hawkins runs the business like a Christian organization. She treats everybody right, treats them equal. But when she say something, she means it. She wants to give good care to the residents, they are her foremost concern, she wants them treated with dignity and respect. As long as you as an employee follow in that pattern, you all right with her. But when you don't treat her patients right, then that's when she can be stern.

When I first came, we had about 45 residents. We were licensed for 76, and with Dr. Hawkins in charge, it did not take long for us to just move up and gain more residents until these 76 beds mostly would stay full. Because of the older neighborhood that we're in, it has always been a good business. Right now we have room for 91 residents.

WILLIE ARNOLD: (Tiny's grandson)
It's been real nice, the people that you get to know

One of my favorite residents was a guy by the name of Ed Jones. He was in a wheelchair, had club feet. But he was so nice to me. Of all the grandkids, he would always ask me, "Could you push me down here?" He'd tell me all kind of stories and give me Fred Flintstone stickers and bubble gum. I can remember pushing him down the halls and just having a lot of fun with him. It's been real nice, the people that you get to know.

RODNEY HAWKINS: (Tiny's younger son)
Everybody here has their favorite patient

I don't know why that is, but we all have our pick. Mother loves everybody here, but she's got her favorites, too. Right now, her favorite patient is Mary Clemens. Mother had her moved up there right across from her office. That's where she puts her favorites. Mary has Alzheimer's, but she still knows Miss Hawkins right away when she sees her.

Dave, he's my favorite patient right now, that's my buddy. He used to be a vagrant, live

---

MATTIE HELEN SAMUELS: (Tiny's niece)
She is employing people in the neighborhood

Most of our employees are from this neighborhood, and they can walk to work. They live right here in South Dallas within one to 12 blocks. Because the nursing home industry has such a low wage scale, it's hard to get people who would have to catch buses to work here. The bus fare is so high. There's a large turnover in staff. That's not unusual for the industry. I've seen a lot of people come and go.

DON BRODEN: (Tiny's grandson)
Dr. Hawkins provides jobs for people

A lot of those working here are not making top dollar, but they're making something. If some people don't work, they'll be criminals. She's keeping people working, keeping them in society, keeping them going. So maybe they don't have to be on welfare. I think her biggest contribution is she employs people when she doesn't have to.

on the street. He doesn't talk much. He stayed here for eight years and did not say a word. But now he talks to me. I'll say, "How's it going, Dave?" "Fine." And I say, "Well what do you need, buddy?" And he'd reply, "Cigarette." And I say, "Okay."

Yeah, I just like him, the way he grins at me when he knows he's done something he's not supposed to do. The employees often get mad at him because he'll go in the break room and take their lunch and eat it. He just tickles me. He knows he can't smoke in the building. And sometimes we'll be outside, and I'll give him a cigarette, and he'll get up and start walking toward the building with the cigarette, and I say, "Dave, now you know you can't go in." "Oh, yeah." Then he'll turn around and sit back down.

I've had others that have passed, like Carnell Milton, she used to be my favorite patient. She would come up to me every day and dance with me. She'd tell me, "You know, I love you." I say, "I love you, too."

I don't think Mother will ever not work over here. I think it helps her because she always says, "I may get old, old, old, but I'm not going to lose my mind." I think working here keeps her sharp, mentally alert, mentally focused. It makes her happy, it really does.

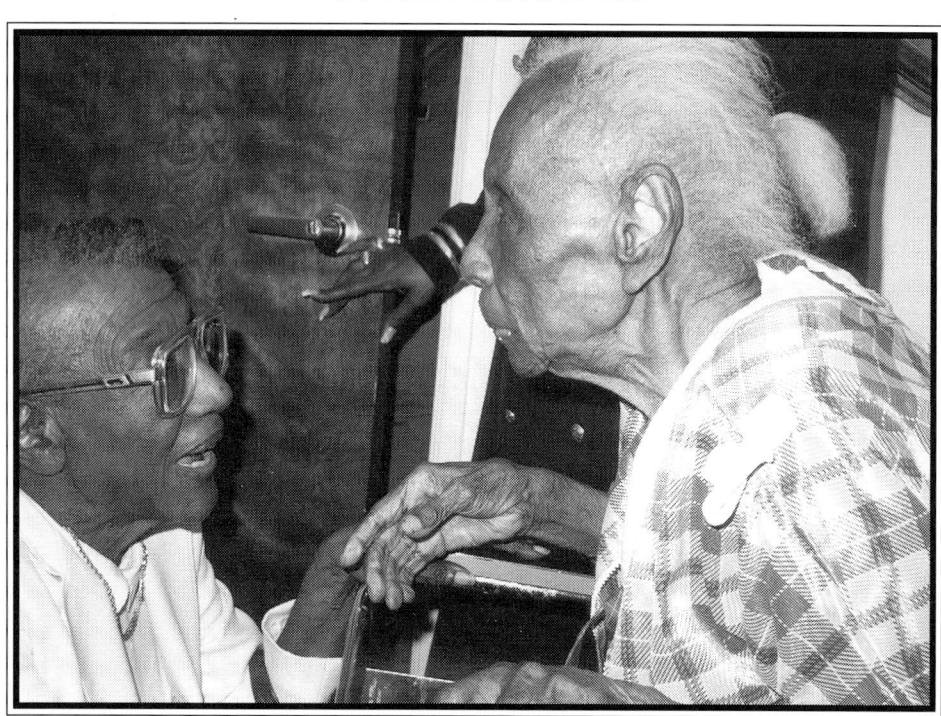

My sister, Evelyn Livingston, with my aunt, Arelia Hunter. Aunt Arelia was 106 here.

TINY AND RODNEY

Mother tells us, "Just go on and do it," and we usually do.
"I'm over here seven days a week, ten and twelve hours a day.
Now, ya'll could come over here on some of these weekends to cover for me."
Of course, me and Rod would rather be in front of the TV this weekend with
a bucket of hot wings and a beer looking at the football game.

BURT HAWKINS

I told the bank,
"You need to let me have the money in this community
just about as bad as I need it.
So, if you don't let me have it, you may see 12 beds on one corner and
12 wheelchairs on one corner and six beds on the other corner. And
I'll call Channel 4, 5, and 8 and tell them
to come out and see how the other half live."

CHAPTER TEN

I WOULDN'T GIVE UP

*The bank let me have this money but they
didn't really want me to have it.
And they pulled a lot of stunts,
but I called their hand on all of them.*
Tiny Hawkins

TINY HAWKINS:

A spotless nursing home

Rodney's right, it has made me happy being here. But in 1980, I had paid off the place and proved my doubters wrong. They had said it couldn't be done, but I said, "Uh, huh, I did it." But I was just bored stiff coming to work every day, and it wasn't a challenge to me anymore. After 20 years, I decided to retire. That lasted about six months, and I was more bored at home. So I came back to work.

By then we were spending a lot of money for the upkeep of the building because it was real old. We kept the nursing home real clean, and everybody was just amazed at how clean it was and how it smelled. But we were spending too much money.

Between the state and the Medicare people, someone would show up to inspect us every three months. Every inspection, I'd have to spend several thousand dollars. You either had to put in a new fire alarm system, or you had to put in a nurse call system, or you had to bring it up to some type of standard.

So I just said one day, "What the heck. I may as well just redo this whole thing. I'm spending all this money anyhow, and I'm not doing anything but patchin'. So I just might as well bite the bullet." Well, them folks at the bank didn't want to give me that money. It took me over two years to get a loan.

TINY HAWKINS:

**They gave a white guy
two million dollars**

I had to threaten the financial institution with a lot of things. I knew a white guy 46 years old who had borrowed two million dollars just like that for a business that hadn't been established as long as mine. He didn't have as much going for him as I had, and he told me, "I will go with you."

He told me I could use his name, and I did. I threatened them with that, too. It took me over two years to get the money — really, I started long before then. I started about five years prior. And then I just dropped it. And then all of a sudden I said, "I'll be darned if I let them get away with this."

There was one white lady at the bank that worked with me; she was really on my side but her boss wasn't, and I knew it. I told him to his face, I just said everything to him that I thought about saying and told him just how I felt.

And another young black guy, Mr. Charles English, from the South Dallas Development Corporation put up half a million dollars, too. He was at a meeting with me one day at the bank, just sipping his coffee.

And I said something, and he was shocked. When we got downstairs he said, "Lady, I don't know who you are, but I have never had nobody to come across the way you came across." Me and him and my son Burt was the only blacks at the meeting.

He said, "You read that man so until he turned red as a beet." I said, "Well, I was telling the truth." And I just told them.

TINY HAWKINS:
They just didn't want to let me have that money

I told the bank, "You need to let me have the money in this community just about as bad as I need it. So, if you don't let me have it, you may see 12 beds on one corner and 12 wheelchairs on one corner and six beds on the other corner. And I'll call Channel 4, 5, and 8 and tell them to come out and see how the other half live." And they looked surprised.

Then every time they started dragging their feet a little bit, I'd come up with some other kind of threat until finally I got it. And then they really didn't give me enough to do what I wanted to do, but at least I got enough to remodel. They don't really want me to tell the whole story about 'em.

They let me have this money, but they didn't really want me to have it. And they pulled a lot of stunts, but I called their hand on all of them. That's the reason why I think they were afraid not to give me the money, for fear of what I might say if they didn't let me have it.

TINY HAWKINS:
We're having a ribbon-cutting Friday

We had the grand opening September 25, 1995. The bank sponsored it, but I had to threaten them on that, too. I said, "Now, I don't have any money for the opening. I owe you all, and I'll never pay you off before I die.

But y'all made sure you'll get paid because you got some life insurance that will back you up in case something happen to me. And I need to fill this place up, so you all need to come on out here and make the opening a success.

Do what you going do. I'm just going be here lookin' pretty." They got the invitations out. They did it all.

You all need to come on out here and make the opening a sucess is what I told the bank.

BURT SAMUEL HAWKINS: (Tiny's older son)
If it's God's will

In 1989, I told Dr. Hawkins, "We got to do something." We was spending $40,000-50,000 dollars on maintenance on the old building. "We could use this money instead toward a brand new facility. That would mean more beds and make us more money."

Dr. Hawkins said, "It sounds like a good idea. You put a plan together, and if we can get a loan, well, then I'll do it." First time we tried, the bank wouldn't give us enough money. She said, "Well, don't stop now. Just keep working." And the next time, all the projections that I gave the bank hit within a couple hundred dollars.

They put a package together, and we got it done. I tend to think that there was some blatant racism, because of some of the dogged stipulations of things that we had to do that I don't feel would normally have been required. The bank gave us a book this thick.

We got about the same amount of money from the South Dallas Development Corporation without near those stipulations. The way Dr. Hawkins taught me to think, "If it's God's will for us to get something, then irregardless of racism, it's going to be done."

TINY HAWKINS:
Attorney Stanley Kaufman never took a dime

Stanley Kaufman was the attorney for the nursing home even before I bought it. Then when I took it over, I was well acquainted with him because I had worked closely with him in the past because the previous owner was never there.

I asked him would he be the attorney for the nursing home. He laughed and said, "You can't afford me. But I'll take you on as a client. I think you're a wonderful person, and we work together real well."

From that day forward, he handled all my legal work. He never took a dime because he knew I couldn't afford to pay him. And I told him I didn't like charity, and when I paid the place off, he'd get the next note. And anytime I had a little money, I'd mail him a check. But he would never cash it.

When we paid for the nursing home, I sent him another check, and he still didn't take it. I finally sent it to his secretary and told her, "You deposit this money and don't tell Stanley."

So that's how I was able to pay him. He was one of three or four persons who said I could be a success at the nursing home business.

His son, Aaron Kaufman, still represents the South Dallas Nursing Home, and that's been

Anytime I had a little money, I'd mail Stanley a check. But he would never cash it.

almost 30 years, and the family is real near and dear to my heart because they helped me be where I am today.

YVONNE HAWKINS HERVEY: (Tiny's fourth daughter)
The future of nursing homes

The nursing home is such a complicated business. If Congress takes away any more funding from the elderly, I just don't see how they can survive. What they anticipate doing is children taking care of their elderly parents. Baby boomers like me might be on Social Security or disability ourselves by that time. They want us to pay for our parents' health care. I don't think it's going to work at all. The majority of people are not going to be able to take care of their parents.

It's going to make it difficult for nursing homes like ours to stay in business, difficult for us to pay people, get people to work. The cost of living is too high now for us to take a cut in reimbursements. We pay a little bit more than the average wage, but the high turnover goes along with the lack of funds. Most health care workers don't have any benefits of their own. We have an HMO for our workers, but most of them really can't even afford to pay their share. They just can't afford it.

MATTIE HELEN SAMUELS: (Tiny's niece)
A facelift for South Dallas

You know, South Dallas has been labelled a bad place, a ghetto part of town. Dr. Hawkins wanted to show people that it doesn't have to be like that. It can be nice just like any other area in Dallas. South Dallas needs a face lift. They're tearing down all that rubbish and clearing it up, and I take my hat off to them. I hate to see anything fall down.

All it takes is people to work together and to build it up and make it look better. And in making a place look better, people will draw to you more.

I nominated Dr. Hawkins for the National
Black Women Who Made it Happen Award.
I told the judges how Dr. Hawkins took over this nursing home business
with a $500,000 indebtedness and cleared the debt.
It was a big thrill for all of us.
She won during our National Convention.

LILY GREEN

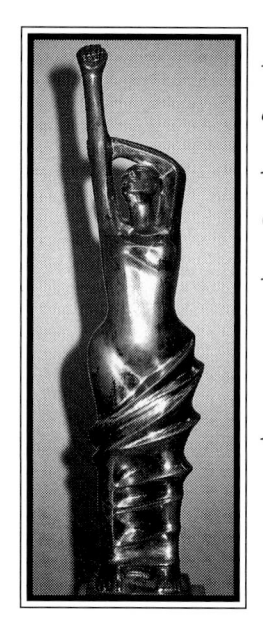

Frito-Lay and NCNW Salute Black Women Who Make It Happen

Leona Hawkins

We salute you as a woman of exceptional achievement. Your dedication to community service, your determination to correct injustice, and your ability to overcome obstacles have improved quality of life for many and have put success within easier reach for Black women.

President, Frito-Lay
November 15, 1985

President, NCNW
November 15, 1985

CHAPTER ELEVEN

LEAVE NO ONE BEHIND

*The National Council of Negro Women
has been an organization that I have always been proud of.
It doesn't exclude anyone.*
Tiny Hawkins

TINY HAWKINS:
I served as president for 13 years

The second section of the National Council of Negro Women, the Oak Cliff section, was organized in Dallas in 1975. A group of ladies, about ten or 12 of us, came together to organize a Council in the City of Dallas. We already had one, the Metro section, and we were organizing the second section.

The first president was Ruth McGee. Ella Hill was elected the second vice, and I was the third vice. After Ruth McGee served a year, Ella Hill became the second president; she served about a year-and-a-half, and then I served as president for 12 years. I became president in 1979; served until 1991.

TINY HAWKINS:
We exclude no one

As president, I went to almost all of the district, state, and national conventions. All our national meetings were held in Washington, D.C., every two years. That's where we would meet up with people from all over the United States.

The National Council of Negro Women has been an organization that I have always been proud of. It is made up of 30 separate organizations. One of the main reasons why I love the National Council of Negro Women is because it does not segregate. It is an organization of organizations which doesn't exclude anyone.

The only question we ask you is, "Do you want to help somebody?" Any woman can join, whether she has a third grade education or a college education. That is why it has been my priority, because so often, women are excluded from an organization because of the lack of education or their background. One of our national themes is to "Leave No One Behind," and that's one of my philosophies, too.

TINY HAWKINS:
We work on important social issues

We started out with about 15 members and then we increased the membership to about 50. Then under my administration, the membership increased to 219 members.

Any issues that faced women we addressed,

whether it was school issues, teenage pregnancy, juvenile delinquents, the job place, any of the things that would make for a better community. We had 20-25 committees with about eight or ten people on each one.

TINY HAWKINS:
Pregnant girls were not forgotten

We organized state-wide. We were awarded about $30,000 to run this program, to teach our young people, the young girls and the boys, too. They were just beginning to talk about sex education in the schools.

We went to schools, we nurtured different teenagers who got pregnant. We'd buy them clothes. For teenagers away from home who came into the city without anything, we always had a storehouse where we were able to give them some clothes, sheets, pillowcases, and start them out where they could get a job.

I remember one South Dallas teenager we helped. I gave her a job at the nursing home while she was still in high school. We entered her into a contest and helped her get a scholarship. She later finished high school and two years at El Centro Junior College and was able to raise her baby with the help of her mother.

Most of the pregnant teenagers just really didn't know what they were getting off into. We had classes to teach them how to take care of themselves and the babies. We would teach them personal hygiene, poise, etiquette, charm, anything to make them feel good about themselves and how to raise them babies.

We had politicians, we had nurses, we had administrators, we had homemakers in the organization to help these young women. The

Tiny with Barbara Bush and Dorothy Height at Blair House in Washington, D.C.

nurses would teach them about birth control. We had people who were in business teach them how to go off into business. Beauticians would teach them charm, grace.

TINY HAWKINS:
My bio was only six inches long

In 1985, I was in the top 15 national finalists of those being considered for the Black Women Who Made It Happen Award, sponsored by Frito Lay and the National Council of Negro Women.

We all had to go to Washington, D.C., to see who were going to be the five women that received these awards.

The editor of **Essence** magazine was on the screening panel, along with Vice President George Bush's wife, Barbara Bush, and several other women. Nobody knew me.

They only went by a short biographical sketch, about six inches long, sent in by my friend Lily Green. And the other 14 finalists had a bio about four feet long.

Three or four of my kids came to Washington for the ceremony. The night before the banquet where we were to receive the awards I had my picture made with this bronze award statue by Elizabeth Catlett, a leading black sculptress. I said, "This is as close to this statue as I'll ever get, so y'all come on and take my picture." And they did.

And the next night at the banquet, I was just shocked because I was one of the five finalists. I couldn't even get up out of my chair.

Here I am with Dorothy Height and other finalists

About twelve of us organized the Oak Cliff Section of
The National Council of Negro Women in Dallas in 1976

81

We all serve God and we live for God.
And we all have patience with everybody and try to love everybody.
Be encouraged, be strong because trouble don't last always.
We've been through some rough times.

GRADUATING CLASS OF SOUTHERN BIBLE INSTITUTE

CHAPTER TWELVE

MY STRENGTH IS IN GOD

*She is the ram in the bush
that holds this family together*
Portia Samuels

TINY HAWKINS:
My daddy was a preacher

My daddy, Frank Mathis, had the most influence on me. He was a preacher. He built the Glasco Chapel AME Church in Kemp where he was the minister. I can remember crawling up in the pulpit when I was small. Getting up there, sitting in my daddy's lap.

PORTIA SAMUELS: (Tiny's great-niece)
She sat on the pulpit with her father

I remember Evelyn, Tiny's sister, telling me about how Grandpa Frank would go up to the pulpit and he would take Tiny with him. She sat up there with him, and he said that she was a special child.

EMMA JEAN WHITE: (Tiny's oldest sister)
She was always right

She always wanted to be right. She never argued about anything. She'd say, "Well I'm right, and I'm going do it." She usually did it. But we were a family, whatever one wanted to do, we didn't dis-encourage each other.

We always stuck by for them to do it. We would help all that we knew how to. We'd pray for one another and wanted each other to be strong in Christ Jesus. So far, it has always come

The St. Paul A.M.E. Church Usher Board No. 2

out like that. I don't know a one of us who is not Christian people, not a one.

We all serve God and we live for God. And we all have patience with everybody and try to love everybody. 'Cause God isn't going to ask that person, "What did you do?" He's going to always ask me, "What did I do?"

ETHEL LIVINGSTON: (Tiny's older sister)
Tiny was her favorite

Our Aunt Arelia Freeman always planned programs at her church — the Oak Grove Baptist Church — in Kemp. She always wanted Tiny on her program because Tiny was her favorite. She said she thought Tiny was the prettiest thing she ever saw.

TINY HAWKINS:
I used to give speeches all the time

I used to do a lot of public speaking in church. I never charged, I never had a fee. People would want me to come and speak for

St. Paul Groundbreaking — Be encouraged, be strong, because trouble don't last always

their missionary society or their clubs or their organizations.

I'm a member of the St. Paul AME Church on Metropolitan and Latimer which is part of the Texas Tenth Episcopal District, AME Church. These days I don't speak as much of the time as I used to. I used to speak an awful lot.

ETHEL LIVINGSTON: (Tiny's older sister)
My husband's been pastor there for 55 years

I grew up in the Methodist church, but I married a Baptist minister, Forest L. Livingston. F.L. has been the Baptist pastor of the Greater St. John Church around the corner on Metropolitan and Atlanta for 55 years.

LILY GREEN: (Bookkeeper and long-time friend)
Long live Miss Hawkins

Tiny is a member of St. Paul AME Church right here on Metropolitan. She's a very Christian woman. God is her motivator. He's her strength. I'm sure there's been times during these 20-some years at the nursing home that she could have given up, but she had that inner strength to go on and do more.

There's a saying, "Long Live the Queen." Well, I say, "Long Live Miss Hawkins." I don't know what it would be like without her. She keeps everybody on their toes. "You've got to do this, and you've got to do that." She's the type of person that motivate you to do what you have to do. Miss Hawkins has a way of keeping you in line. I have gained strength from her in many, many instances. She's been there for me.

KEVIN WESLEY: (Tiny's grandson)
A circle of joined hands

Any time there would be a family crisis or argument, my grandmother stressed the importance of God, religion. She said, "The family that prays together stays together." "Uncle Morris, you say a prayer." She'd make sure that even, just for this one day,

"Let's all sit down or stand in a circle and join hands."

BURT HAWKINS: (Tiny's older son)
Her day starts with God

That's Dr. Hawkins' basis, that's where she gets her strength. That's where we all get our sense of fair play and our sense of what our place is. She instilled it in each and every one of us that your day starts with God.

If I'm not right with God, well, then, the rest of my day is not going to be right. So I have to keep that relationship straight before I keep the relationship with my wife and my kids and with my job and my parents and my family.

This didn't click in my head until I was about 28 years old. I used to think, "Hell, I might live forever," but then it just clicked, "I could be gone tomorrow and where am I going to be then?"

One of her other things is, "Be encouraged, be strong, because trouble don't last always." And we've been through some rough times.

That is where I get my strength from everyday to come over here to the nursing home, because some days I just really don't feel like coming.

WILLIE ARNOLD, JR.: (Tiny's grandson)
Every day she keeps turning it over to God

I think she's been so successful because of

I've learned to celebrate the good times.
You never know what's waiting around the corner.

her spiritual background, her wholehearted believing in God. But there's also her stubbornness, her willingness to say, "And, well, nobody else has done it this way. I'm going to do it this way. My way or no way." At the same time, she has that gentleness. These are some of the keys to her success.

PORTIA SAMUELS: (Tiny's great niece)
**She is the ram in the bush
that holds this family together**

I know that God works through people, and He works through her. She's just always been special to me. As an adult I've really gotten to know her and spend more time with her than I did when I was young.

RODNEY HAWKINS: (Tiny's younger son)
She is very, very religious

She bases everything on her relationship with God. And from there, you can see her spirit. She's very God-like, the way she deals with people and the way she deals with everybody. She's very fair. She's a real nice person.

SANDRA HAWKINS BRODEN: (Tiny's second daughter)
Her strength is in God

Anybody who has a problem even to this day calls her. But she doesn't have anyone to call. Her strength is in God.

JULIETTE HAWKINS WESLEY: (Tiny's third daughter)
Hard times and good times

Our family road has not been a crystal staircase. We've touched on all the wonderful things and all the success stories, but there have been hard times, too. Because we're a strong family the bad times didn't derail us. Even at the lowest point, the most troublesome, there's been one family member who has maintained the others.

The strength that Mother had to keep her sisters and brothers and children and nieces and nephews and grandchildren together — I find myself doing that, too, to keep that structure going. Every generation has a new set of problems, but because the family values have been instilled, I can't give up.

I can't say I've done all I can, or I've gone my last mile. Sometimes when I think I can't go any further, Mother is always standing there going, "You can, and you will! You'll do whatever it takes, you won't let go. You can, you will, and you'll be fine.

WILLIE ARNOLD, JR.: (Tiny's grandson, Yvonne's son)
**Following in my
grandmother's footsteps**

My grandmother instilled values in my mother which my mother passed on to me. Sometimes I would talk to my grandmother

Willie Arnold, Jr. and Willie Arnold, III

because she could always tell if something was actually eating at me. She would say, "Well, come in and talk to me. How you doing today?"

In our family, my grandmother has been like the big Rock of Gibraltar — she's always there, strong, stable. I've never seen a time when she panicked at a crisis. It's always, "Let go and let God. Well, so be it. Whatever happens, happens, and it'll work itself out. "Family first and foremost. Being the strong backbone in the family. If one of your family members needs you, it's top priority. When somebody's ever needed me, I've always been the one: "Will, something's going on. We need you." Five or six minutes later, I'm there.

TINY HAWKINS:
**I owe it all to my parents
and to my faith in God**

Well, I've had good times and I've had bad times. I've had to be so strong for so many for so long, sometimes it seems like more than I can bear. I've tried to live my life by the Golden Rule: it is more blessed to give than to receive.

The secret to her success is her heart.
She really cares about people. It's something you got to be born with.
You got to have a good heart. If you don't have a good heart,
nothing will go right for you. Her heart's really right, and
her faith in her religion is right.

PASTORS
REV. FRANK L. MATHIS, MY FIRST MINISTER
REV. DRINKARD TIMMS, REV. JAMERSON, REV. E. L. WRIGHT
REV. DAVID F. HARRIS, REV. B. L. McCORMICK, REV. W. E. CARTER

We are the music makers,
And we are the dreamers of dreams
Yet we are the movers and shakers
Of the world for ever, it seems.
THE HAWKINS FAMILY

Charlotte, Juliette, Burt, Yvonne, Sandra
Rodney, Sam, Tiny

EPILOGUE

STRONG FAMILY TIES
The Tiny Hawkins Story

Tiny Hawkins is a woman of power, a woman of action, and a woman to be remembered. She exemplifies the honor, dignity, and spirit of the best humanity has to offer.
Debra Winegarten

"I believe in strong family ties," is one of the first things Tiny Hawkins said to me. As I met her sisters, aunts, sons, daughters, nieces, nephews, grandchildren and "greats" parading through her office of the South Dallas Nursing Home, I began to get a feel for what she meant.

Family is first and foremost for Tiny. The ninth of 12 children, she embodies holding all God's children as part of her family. The people living at her nursing home receive the same love and care as her mother and other family members who ended their days there. Tiny's children, most of whom work alongside her, hold Tiny's philosophy of "strong family ties" as their own.

Tiny early on turned her back on picking cotton and cleaning white women's kitchens to become a self-employed businesswoman. Using the entrepreneurial skills learned from her father, she made her kitchen into a beauty shop. Tiny in action at her nursing home is a larger version of the kitchen, with the phone ringing, people coming in, Tiny directing the staff and talking to the residents, all at the same time. Tiny Hawkins doesn't need a flow chart — she does what needs to be done, juggling many balls in the air at the same time.

Tiny's deep spiritual side is reflected not only in her commitment to and being a leader in her church, it is also shown each day in her connection with the residents. "Missionary work is personal to me, I do it on a daily basis." For Tiny, God is present in each person she comes in contact with, and she finds that spark, however small, and blows on it until the flame blazes forth. She turns to God many times a day for strength, and relies on her faith to get her through each day.

Each of Tiny's family members (except the very youngest) made some reference to the twig story, either recounting it directly, or talking about the interweaving, tying, bonding strength of this family. Clearly, the metaphor of the twig story binds this family together.

Tiny has built a vibrant business in the heart of South Dallas, traditionally one of the poorest sections of the city. The Dallas skyline is visible from the front porch of the nursing home, which provides stable employment and viability in an area undergoing urban renewal. Tiny's vision has built a business not only to support herself and her family, but the entire neighborhood and community, as well.

Signs of rebirth in the neighborhood include the African American Museum of Dallas, which preserves not only Tiny's history, but that of other prominent Texans, as well.

A woman who won't take no for an answer, Tiny Hawkins gets what she wants. Using perserverence, a sly wit, and a calculated risk, Tiny and her children have built a two million dollar enterprise which is a gift to the South Dallas Community.

The first person in her family to go to college, Tiny took continuing education units until the administration informed her it was time to write her dissertation. "I never intended on getting my doctorate," she told me, "I just kept taking those 3 and 6-hour continuing education courses, and before I knew it, I had my doctorate."

Tiny urges her grandchildren, "Go to school, go to school, go to school. "I believe in the value of education, I knew the only way for me to get out of that hot sun was to go to school, and I never wanted to have to pick cotton again." Tiny's slave grandparents would be proud of the amazing empire she has built in just two generations.

Tiny's political life stretches from work with the National Council of Negro Women, to registering voters, to campaigning and advising politicians she believes in.

Weaving different aspects of her life together, she has served on national boards for her church, as president of the Ushers Society, completed Bible College, and is a popular public speaker for local churches and organizations.

Dr. Tiny Hawkins has gone only 30 miles down the road from a modest farm in the country town of Kemp to Dallas, but the journey is rich with inspiration and hard work, a sterling example of a woman achieving against all odds.

This remarkable woman is a quiet tornado. Being around her is like being in the calm in the eye of a storm. Tiny Hawkins is a woman of power, a woman of action, and a woman to be remembered. She exemplifies the honor, dignity, and spirit of the best humanity has to offer.

Sandra Hawkins Broden and her family

Join us now in celebration of the six generations of
human courage and dignity you have in your hands.
In this book, secrets are revealed of survival,
prosperity, ingenuity, management, strategies, extrication,
prevention, economics, racism, class mobility,
education, self-esteem, values, human relationships,
employment, self-employment, mentorship and love.

OUR THANKS TO DR. TINY HAWKINS

That's the way family ties are.
Whatever happens to you kids, always stick together.
When one is down, the other needs to be there
to pick that one up.

JULIETTE HAWKINS WESLEY AND HER FAMILY

CHRONOLOGY

STRONG FAMILY TIES
The Tiny Hawkins Story

1952	Received Negro Achievement Award, National Negro Magazine.
1958-60	Graduated Madame C.J. Walker Beauty College, Instructor.
1960-68	Self-employed — instructor/operator, cosmetology.
1963	"Mother of the Year" award, Lincoln High School
	President, Lincoln High PTA — four years.
1968-69	Director of Social Services, South Dallas Nursing Home.
1969-74	Assistant Administrator, South Dallas Nursing Home.
1970	647th individual to be licensed in Texas as a Nursing Home Administrator, first black to be licensed in the state.
1974	Purchased South Dallas Nursing Home from Jack Counts, assumed $500,000 note.
1975	One of the founders of the National Council of Negro Women, Oak Cliff Branch.
1977	Samuel Hawkins died.
	Attended San Jacinto College, Pasadena, Texas.
	Preceptor, Nursing Home Administration.
1979-91	Became third president of National Council of Negro Women chapter, Oak Cliff.
1981	Zeta Woman of the Year.
1985	Frito-Lay and National Council of Negro Women, "Salute to Black Women Who Make it Happen" Award, Washington, DC (one of five awardees, nationwide).
1986	Museum of African American Life & Culture, Dallas.
	Texas Black Women's Hall of Fame & Exhibit.
	Featured in Frito-Lay "Celebration of Achievement" Learning Kit.
1987	Retired as Administrator of South Dallas Nursing Home.
	Returned to work after six months.
	One of Quest for Success Awardees (Miller Brewing Company, Dallas Black Chamber of Commerce, Dallas Morning News).
	Dallas Morning News High Profile article (May 31).
1988	Earned Doctorate of Business Administration degree from Pacific Western

University, 600 N. Sepulveda, Los Angeles, CA 90049.
Juanita Craft Award, Dallas NAACP Business Award.

1991 Dallas Black Living Legends, Junior Black Academy.
1992-95 Attended Southern Bible Institute.
1995 Opened remodeled South Dallas Nursing Home, September 23.
1996 Sandra joined staff of South Dallas Nursing Home.

Burt Hawkins and his family

Four generations of the Mathis family

I just didn't want no kids,
but I wouldn't take a million dollars for them.
You don't think about living to 106.
You don't think about grandkids growing up
and having kids who never knew you.
DERRICK AND KEVIN WESLEY

RUTHE WINEGARTEN AND DEBRA WINEGARTEN

Tiny Hawkins' story needed telling.
The Winegartens stepped in and made it happen.
They have driven back and forth from Austin to Dallas to
interview friends and relatives and provide their
expertise in documentation and editing, and
just having fun in this undertaking.
Thank you cannot adequately express what we feel.

SANDRA HAWKINS BRODEN

BIBLIOGRAPHY

STRONG FAMILY TIES
The Tiny Hawkins Story

Barr, Alwyn. (1996). Black Texans: A History of African Americans in Texas, 1528-1971, 2nd Ed., University of Oklahoma Press: Norman, OK.

Charlton, Thomas L. (1985). Oral History for Texans, 2nd Ed., Texas Historical Commission: Austin, TX.

Craft, Juanita. (1982). A Child, the Earth, and a Tree of Many Seasons: The Voice of Juanita Craft. Halifax Publishing: Dallas, TX.

Denzin, Norman K. (1989). Interpretive Biography. Sage Publications, Inc.: Newbury Park, CA.

Gee, Sadye, comp. and Williams, Darnell, Ed. (1986). Black Presence in Dallas, Historic Black Dallasites. Museum of African-American Life and Culture: Dallas, TX.

Hill, Patricia Evridge. (1996). Dallas: The Making of a Modern City. University of Texas Press: Austin, TX.

Kirk, Jerome and Miller, Marc L. (1986). Reliability and Validity in Qualitative Research. Sage Publications, Inc.: Beverly Hills, CA.

Mills, C. Wright. (1959). The Sociological Imagination. Oxford University Press: New York.

Museum of African American Life and Culture. (1986). They Showed the Way: An Exhibit of Black Texas Women, 1836-1986. MAALC: Dallas, TX.

Nance, Sharon. (1992). Doctoral Dissertation on "Technological Adaptation Strategies among Minority Black Farm Workers." The Ohio State University: Columbus, OH.

Robinson, Dorothy. (1991). "Interview with Juanita Craft." Jan. 20, 1977 in The Black Women Oral History Project, v. 3:12-15. K.G. Saur Verlag, a Reed Reference Publishing Co., and the Arthur and Elizabeth Schlesinger Library. Radcliffe College.

Winegarten, Ruthe. (1997). Black Texas Women: 150 Years of Trial and Triumph, 2nd Ed. University of Texas Press: Austin, TX.

_____. (1996). Black Texas Women: A Source Book. University of Texas Press: Austin, TX.

_____. (1996). I Am Annie Mae: An Extraordinary Black Texas Woman In Her Own Words. University of Texas Press: Austin, TX.

Oral Interviews

Arnold, Willie Jr.
Broden, Don
Broden, Scott
Broden, Morris Rev.
Broden, Sandra Hawkins
Dillworth, Evelyn Mathis
Finley, Mark
Finley, Mona
Flewellen, Leola Mathis
Green, Lily
Hawkins, Rodney
Hawkins, Samuel (Burt), Jr.
Hawkins, Dr. Leona "Tiny" Mathis
Hervey, Yvonne Hawkins
Hunter, Arelia Freeman
Livingston, Ethel Mathis
Mathis, Frank, Jr.
Nelson, Ann Mathis
Samuels, Mattie Helen
Samuels, Portia
Siruis, Chris
Wesley, Juliette Hawkins
Wesley, Kevin
White, Emma Jean Mathis

Design

Starinsky Studios
Woodland Park, Colorado

Tamara Hawkins, daughter of Burt Hawkins,
granddaughter of Tiny Hawkins

*Whatever assistance is needed at any moment, inspiration,
direction, zeal, enthusiasm, will, determination,
it is provided by the power of God.
Doubt and uncertainty have no power over me.
We all work together to share in the beauty,
to be a part of the plan.*

TINY HAWKINS